Swimming
with
Dolphins

Susan Dawson-Cook, M.S.

Swimming with Dolphins
Copyright © 2022 Susan Dawson-Cook
Published by Corazon del Oro Communications, LLC
Cover Art by Anya Kelleye
Front Cover Photo by Pam Hopkins
Back Cover Photo by Fred Elling
ISBN: 9798846564220

Swimming with Dolphins celebrates the world of water, which has been my training ground for personal and spiritual growth, and, throughout my life, a constant source of renewal and joy. It celebrates my unique friendship and interactions with a group of bottlenose dolphins in San Carlos, México, and explores their intelligence, resourcefulness, and playfulness. This memoir draws on my experiences living as an expatriate and recounts how this life change enhanced my health and spiritual growth. It mourns the destruction man inflicts on animal habitats and the diverse creatures that share our planet. I call upon my readers to be mindful and responsible, and to protect and defend the wildlife that surrounds us, no matter where we live.

PREFACE

San Carlos, México – August 2017

"Some people crave illicit substances when upset: my drug of choice is saltwater." Susan Casey – *Voices in the Ocean: A Journey into the Wild and Haunting World of Dolphins*

My life could be divided into three parts—before I found the water, after I found the water, and my later-in-life discovery of sea swimming. Childhood days spent on dry land were difficult. Because I was picked on and bullied, I often felt like a victim, weak and powerless. I was like a caught fish, flopping around until eighth grade, when my friend Karen invited me to join the swim team. In the water, I thrived. When I discovered sea swimming—and the dolphins that reign in this realm— well, that's what this story is about.

I've been a swimmer for 46 years now. When I introduce myself, I could as easily say, "I'm a swimmer," as "I'm Susan." Swimming calms me when I'm anxious, balances me when I feel out of kilter, and gives me the strength to cope when I'm in mourning. The water is my sanctuary, the one place I always feel safe. It's also where I feel connected to a Divine presence.

For decades, swimming pools were my training ground, but when my husband and I started living in San Carlos, México, on the Sea of Cortez, I fell in love with open water swimming. Now, after five years of almost daily sea swimming, I find it difficult to return to black lines and flip turns. A chlorinated pool can't compete with the wild unpredictability of the open water. In the sea, I swim for the sheer joy of being in the water. Sea swimming has enabled me to let go of my obsession with competition and worrying about being enough—I can just be. I race in open water from time to time, and even win my age category, but my placing is no longer my priority. Out in the sea, I lose track of time as my body rises and dips with the waves.

I inhale the salt air as I swim—freestyle, breaststroke, or a lazy backstroke. Sometimes I just tread water and look out, awestruck, over the vast expanse of aquamarine sea. Seventy percent of God's beautiful Earth is covered by ocean and sea. What a gift that water is. Gratitude swells in my heart every day I immerse myself in it. The smell and taste and sensation of the salty sea rushing over my skin delivers that multisensory outdoor experience I thrive on, breathes new life into my whole being.

But it is the flash of a dark, wet dorsal fin in the early morning sunlight that raises my heart rate another notch, and that transforms a Sea of Cortez swim from enjoyable to unforgettable.

I first spotted the pod of bottlenose dolphins that I have come to know from my kayak. One dorsal fin surfaced, then suddenly five dolphins breached before diving back into the depths. I stilled my paddling. A few seconds later, I heard loud exhales as the dolphins resurfaced, spewing air and water from their blowholes. A male dolphin dove directly beneath my kayak. My eyes widened, and my pulse pounded when I saw his immense size — the dolphin was at least 10 or 12 feet long. I knew he could overturn my boat with one flick of his powerful tail or fluke.

Instead, the dolphin remained under water until he was well past me before surfacing. I paddled alongside the pod, watching the dolphins' playful jumps and dives and the way they circled around me. It became clear that the dolphins had no harmful intentions. They were curious, just as I was. I watched them with silent wonder, imagining what it would be like to be in the water with them.

One day, I told myself, I would find out.

CHAPTER ONE

Worthington, Ohio – 1970s

"I'd kiss a frog even if there was no promise of a Prince
Charming popping out of it. I love frogs."
Cameron Diaz

I don't remember learning much in elementary school. Only
that I was a misfit. Classmates teased me, and my first reaction
in these instances was to burst into tears. That demonstration
of mental weakness only fueled their desire to torment me. I
had one close friend, Barb. Both of us were tomboys. We spent
hours after school exploring the Olentangy River, catching
frogs, checking out crayfish, and watching the birds dart from
tree to tree.

I grew up in a Christian Science family. I pleaded to God
for help, but despite my prayers, on the school playground,
boys pulled my pants down and called me "Dog doo Dawson."

I'm not saying that Christian Science—or any sincerely held religious belief—can't help. It can and it does. Calling on God to support me with day-to-day problems is normal for me today. I try to listen to God to guide me step by step in my progress. But as a relentlessly-bullied child, I didn't know how to calm my mind to pray or how to apply my Christian Science faith in a time of crisis. I felt very much alone.

 After school, I would rush down to the Olentangy River to cleanse myself of the day's miseries, wading into the river to look for frogs. Back then, they were my favorite wild creatures. Most of the frogs I observed were the Northern Green Frog and the American Bullfrog.

I loved walking to the water's edge and hearing the "eep" sound the frogs made before they leaped into the water with a splash. I'd watch, waiting patiently for the magical moment where two iridescent eyes appeared just above the water, and hope the frog wouldn't submerge again knowing I was near.

With spring came frog mating season. I'd crouch down beside the ponds near the river to observe thousands of wriggling black tadpoles in the shallows. Over weeks, they grew larger and turned olive green and sprung tiny arms and legs. Eventually their tails shrunk away until they were totally transformed into baby frogs.

Few children growing up in today's world will watch tadpoles morph into frogs the way I did. Those ponds and dense forest have since then been replaced by paved bike paths, playgrounds, and soccer fields. Cars and trucks roar along the 315 freeway on the other side of the Olentangy. Frog populations worldwide are being decimated by the chytrid fungus, pesticides, human intrusion, and climate change.

 Bullfrogs, tree frogs (that I often saw clinging to walls outside my grandparents' Florida condo), and leopard frogs played starring roles in my essays and a mystery series I started writing. My fourth-grade teacher, who fawned over the more popular kids, condescendingly informed me that "normal" girls liked horses. "For my own good," she said, she wouldn't accept any more essays about frogs.

I don't often experience violent emotions. But at that moment, every nerve and sinew in my body longed to grab her heavily sprayed hair (that wouldn't move out of place in a hurricane, I'm sure) and rip it from her head by the roots. Writing my thoughts on paper had provided comfort. Writing offered a welcome escape from the world that often seemed hostile to me. It offered an escape I desperately needed.

At least I still had the respite of the Olentangy River. The wild forest and meadows near the river gave me the twin gifts of solitude and safety. There I could escape from people who said I was abnormal, that I didn't belong. Nature never criticized my clothes or indicated that anything about me was lacking. Rather, the hours I spent outside made me feel whole again.

When I was in sixth grade, a high school boy named Bill took an apparent interest in my frog-hunting hobby. He seemed to know when I was at the river alone. One time while I searched for soft-shelled turtles with my younger brother, Dave, Bill approached and said he knew the perfect place. He asked me to accompany him and urged Dave to look somewhere else.

When I waded out of the river, Bill clapped his hand over my mouth, dragged me into the tall grass and yanked hard on my shorts zipper. I was bewildered. And terrified. I screamed, kicked my feet, and frantically tried to push his hands away.

Bill slapped me across the face and told me to shut up. When I continued to flail and scream, he finally let go of me and ran away. I limped home, my body trembling, my clothes wrinkled and muddy, shouting, "I can't take it anymore!"

I hated that my fourth-grade teacher had forbidden me to express myself through my writing. I hated that this high school boy thought I was no more than an object he could do whatever he wanted with. Everyone else seemed to be controlling my life. I wanted to be the one in control. "This has to stop," I muttered, kicking the air, and flinging mud from my shoes.

I told my mother the boy's name and where he lived. Mom scribbled Bill's name on a piece of paper, and set it next to other notes she had collected and, just as quickly, forgotten. I ran upstairs and slammed my room door shut. My mother would be of no help. I dove onto my bed and sobbed.

Looking back, I hold no resentment over what happened. I honestly think Mom didn't believe my horrifying tale. Many years later, I would learn that other girls I knew in Worthington or that grew up during the 1970s elsewhere experienced assault or rape—and their perpetrators weren't confronted either or held accountable in any way. Maybe people didn't want to believe that something so awful could be happening and refused to accept it. Now it is common knowledge this kind of abuse directed at girls and women is an issue and more often it is dealt with. I still often wonder if Bill attacked other girls or women and feel a sense of despair that he wasn't stopped.

I wasn't graced with a hard carapace to retreat into like the river turtles. The only way to protect my vulnerability, to take control of my life, I thought, was to toughen up.

The river's serene beauty couldn't save me from the brutality of others. The water, trees, frogs, and other wild creatures were so beautiful. But this evil human had intruded on my sanctuary and made it feel unsafe.

I clung to the hope that there was some way out. When a friend invited me to join swim team, I thought, yes, that's the answer. I'll eat lots of spinach like Popeye the sailor. I'll become a powerful athlete. I'll build big, strong muscles. And then no one will be able to hurt me again.

After a year of swimming, my body transformed. My thighs broadened, my calves rounded out, and the muscles in my shoulders rippled with newly-developed definition. I walked up and down the school hallways with newfound confidence, swinging my arms athletically, with a clenched-jawed, "don't mess with me" expression on my face. Gloria Gaynor's anthem *I Will Survive* became my personal fight song when I was in high school.

My plan worked. The near constant teasing I had endured for years stopped and kids kept their distance. That's what I wanted. Getting close to people invited danger. I didn't know who I could trust. So, I decided not to trust anyone except my best friend, Barb. I couldn't risk being hurt again.

With swim practices and meets, I didn't have as much time to go to the river anymore. When I went, I'd go with my brother or my next-door neighbor, Jeff.

The pool became my new sanctuary, a refuge where I felt free from the worries and chaos of real life. The first year, I only swam summer league. Then I begged my parents to let me swim year-round. In high school, I practiced before and after school most days. Weekends revolved around meets not only in the greater Columbus area but in Dayton, Cleveland, and Cincinnati.

What I loved most was summer swim season when practices and races were outdoors. I often traveled to meets with other families, sometimes even camping out instead of staying in a hotel. I remember the rolling hills, the green grass, and towering trees in one of the campgrounds near Cincinnati. I remember sleeping on a bunk inside a camper, how we cooked marshmallows for s'mores over a campfire at night. One time we even made doughnuts for breakfast. All the food cooked on the fire tasted amazing. Once my mom and I camped out in the back of our van during a weekend meet.

During the long days of racing, I loved to stretch out my towel in the soft grass under the shade of a tree and read while I waited for my next event to be called. Sometimes, I'd play cards with teammates.

I craved the hours I spent in the water like a drug addict seeking a fix. I didn't care about anything else. While in classes at school, I fantasized about the next workout, the next competition where I'd submerge myself in water all weekend.

I became obsessed by competition, which was like an intoxicating elixir, giving me a sense of power and newfound control over my destiny. I sometimes stood before the mirror with a towel draped loosely across my shoulders. In the reflection stood a powerful Greek goddess. This new muscular me, sculpted by water, wasn't a whiny child at the whim of others any longer. She was strong and athletic and in control. And I found her image to be very empowering.

CHAPTER TWO

San Carlos, México – August-September 2017

"Dolphins are among the smartest creatures on the planet—
fully conscious, creative, and highly communicative, with an
intelligence rare in nature."
Diana Reiss – *The Dolphin in the Mirror*

The water was murky when a huge gray body jetted underneath me. The ominous *Jaws* theme played in my mind. I flashed back to headlines about shark attacks I'd read about swimmers and surfers who had missing limbs or had bled to death. For a moment, fear paralyzed me. Then I shrieked, splashed, and thrashed my way toward shore, sprinting from the water.

"Those aren't sharks," a woman on the beach said, "Those are dolphins."

"Good to know," I answered. I pasted a fake smile on my face and tried to stop hyperventilating.

11

That makes sense, I told myself. Bahía Delfín is the name of our complex. Dolphin Bay. Not Bahía Tiburón or Shark bay.

Whenever I mentioned my dolphin sighting to neighbors or new people I met in town, I'd hear stories about a woman at the Pilar condos who swam with them. "She's been stung by stingrays eight times," one man told me. "The dolphins aren't afraid of her. They swim all around her," another person said. The more stories I heard about this mysterious Danielle, who wore big black flippers and played games with the dolphins, the more I wanted to meet her and have a close encounter with these dolphins myself.

I started scanning the water around me for dolphins whenever I swam. Sometimes I'd see fins arcing over the water from the beach as I waded in. But they never came near me. I wondered if they had sensed my terror during that first encounter and kept their distance out of respect. A month passed, and still I didn't see the dolphins up close.

I learned that the bottlenose dolphins we see near shore in San Carlos are aquatic mammals belonging to the order *Cetacea*, which includes dolphins, porpoises, and whales. These mammals are all warm-blooded, breastfeed their young, and breathe through blowholes on the top of their heads.

I'm not the first person to become entranced by these wild creatures. Dolphins have fascinated humans for centuries. People from ancient Greece, Rome, and the Pacific Islands revered these amazing creatures. And their images appeared everywhere. As dolphin statues. Dolphins stamped into gold coins. I still remember the Bronze Age dolphin fresco my husband and I encountered at Knossos Palace in Crete. The dolphins are blue with white bellies and have fish swimming all around them.

Stories and myths about dolphins and their interactions with humans have been passed down from generation to generation on almost every continent. Diana Reiss's *The Dolphin in the Mirror* regales readers with many of these tales. One recorded in ancient Rome, tells of a young boy whose dolphin friend ferried him across a shallow Naples inlet to and from school every day. After the boy succumbed to an illness, the dolphin continued to look for him every day, and when he never appeared, the dolphin died of sorrow.

People of all cultures continue to have interest in dolphins and follow stories about their interactions and camaraderie with humans. On mornings when I'm headed out to swim, I often see friends I know at our condo complex — Tracey, Bobbe, Nancy, and Sharon gliding by in their kayaks. They're seeking what I'm seeking — one more memorable experience with the dolphins. If you asked any of them about their days around the dolphins on the water, I'm sure they'd regale you with tales equally intriguing as mine. The easiest way for me to captivate people at parties is to share another dolphin tale.

I'll never forget my first up-close encounter with a pod of bottlenose dolphins during a swim. I had raised my head to stay on course and immediately spotted a line of four or five large dorsal fins breaching the surface just a few feet in front of me. Their fins rippled the water before they dove down again. The group of dolphins had covered such a wide swath of water, there was no way to avoid them. They would be underneath me within seconds.

Witnessing their sheer size shot my heart rate way above my aerobic training range. Many of the adult males are 12 feet long and weigh as much as 1,400 pounds. In contrast, I stand five feet four inches and weigh 115 pounds.

They seemed docile enough from the kayak, but what if they're in a bad mood today? It would hurt bad if they tried to bump me out of the way. I held my breath and waited. I'd dreamed of an up-close dolphin encounter for weeks, but now that it was happening, I longed to be safely on shore instead of out here alone with them.

I glanced toward the beach. Maybe they wouldn't run into me intentionally, but what if the dolphins didn't see me? Maybe one would crash into me with a heavy thud. I swam a slow breaststroke, anxiously waiting to see what would happen next. I saw and felt nothing and when I swung my head around, I saw the group of dolphins surface several meters past me. I released a long, relieved breath. They'd obviously been aware of my presence and steered away from me. Did they sense my fear?

I saw the dolphins often on subsequent days. I trusted them the more I swam near them. I'd come a long way since those childhood days where I viewed every person as a potential threat. Now, I savored friendships with people of all ages and was starting to feel Zen calm around these enormous sea creatures.

Reading Susan Casey's *Voices in the Ocean: A Journey into the Wild and Haunting World of Dolphins* gave me even more confidence. I learned that dolphins' echolocation capabilities are superior to the sonar on our country's most sophisticated naval submarines.

Here's the way echolocation works, as I understand it. Dolphins have air sacs beneath their blowholes. Moving air between these air sacs at a rapid rate produces high frequency clicks, each lasting less than a thousandth of a second.

That day, the dolphins didn't come close enough for me to hear their underwater chatter. Dolphins typically emit sounds then listen for echoes from nearby bodies. Their senses are so precise they can determine the size, distance, shape, and the traveling speed of any nearby object—a great asset when they are hunting or trying to avoid collisions with swimmers and motorized crafts. My research and my subsequent encounters

14

led me to believe that the only dolphin collision that would occur would be intentional.

One morning, after about 30 minutes of continuous swimming, I'd reached that blissful in-the-zone state. Suddenly, seven members of the dolphin pod glided directly underneath me. I saw their dorsal fins, their long, sleek bodies, the turned-out tips of their flukes. I forced myself not to blink. If I did, I'd miss seconds of this miracle. The dolphins must have followed me and decided it was time to pass. And the easiest path past was underneath me. My pace must have seemed ridiculously slow compared to the 25-mile-per-hour top speeds their hydrodynamic bodies are capable of.

I've since had dozens of encounters with dolphins from this pod and another one. Each season, new babies are born and taught to catch fish, jump out of the water, and even play. Sometimes they jump for fun. Other times it's to cast off clinging fish, a piece of plastic, or a strand of seaweed.

Male dolphins sometimes swim alone or drift from pod to pod. One male dolphin I've observed seems to be a complete loner. I've never seen him connected to a pod. The large males tend to swim with me more than the others do, occasionally following and circling around me for my entire swim.

Over the course of months and years, these dolphins have become familiar friends. "Good morning. How's it going?" I'll often say in greeting.

Up close, I see their white bellies, the cross patterns of scratches on their blubbery gray and white skin. Algae hangs from the tips of their dorsal fins, their powerful flukes. One dolphin has a pink circle of skin on its head where it collided with a boat propeller. I've named one of the large male dolphins Nick because his dorsal fin is missing a chunk. His fin isn't quite vertical — it skews slightly to one side.

Battle scars help me distinguish between the dolphins. They make each one unique. Nick always swims around with one or two other male dolphins. Often two of them circle around me, whistling and clicking and squeaking before they continue on to their destination with the rest of the pod.

I try to imagine what they're saying when they circle around me, chattering, with perpetual smiles on their faces.

"Oh, that's the new female human swimmer here. Not the woman with big black fins who's usually out here. We can check her out—she's too small to be dangerous."

"Her skin is so white. Like a dead fish floating in the water."

The dolphins swim around me longer during the winter months when the water dips down into the fifties and I'm wearing a wetsuit. I'm guessing they think I'm much more attractive decked out in my sleek black dolphin suit.

CHAPTER THREE

Clemson, South Carolina – June 1983

I swam as a walk-on athlete my freshman year at Clemson. I felt discouraged most of the time during practices. I excelled at breaststroke and freestyle dominated the workouts, so I always fell behind on the intervals. The Clemson coaches didn't provide the atmosphere of fun and encouragement I had been accustomed to with Skip Runkle as coach.

I felt disconnected from my teammates, who seemed obsessed with partying when I preferred to study or pursue outdoor adventure activities on weekends. My swimmer roommate even locked me out of our room once to have sex with her boyfriend. A few swimmers incorrectly concluded that I was gay—since I didn't have a boyfriend or drink my freshman year. I found all this overwhelming.

I kept my distance from them, found other friends, and escaped to the great outdoors, hiking, swimming in Lake Hartwell, white water rafting, and camping in the mountains on weekends. At the end of my freshman year, I quit swimming. The beginning of my sophomore year, I changed my major to geology, which opened up a whole new world of outdoor adventures. On field trips, we collected rock and mineral samples and learned how they were formed. I made some wonderful friends—I loved Mark and David the most—but the geology group tended toward wild and soon I found myself drinking as much as enjoying the great outdoors.

I met a guy related to someone my dad knew from his sailing club. He wasn't a good fit for me, but we dated for more than a year. I occasionally attended the Christian Science Church near Clemson in Seneca. Sometimes, after the service I went to the home of one church member for a group lunch. Everyone was kind and welcoming, but they weren't the life of the party. Then, I just wanted to leave and get back to my fun.

I stopped practicing Christian Science after I became hospitalized with Rocky Mountain Spotted Fever—a very rare and tick-borne disease—during summer school. It all started when aches and fever assaulted me. I walked back to my dorm room dreading the weekend. Being sick in an uncomfortable environment would be miserable. The roommate I'd been assigned for the summer seemed to radiate bad juju. I didn't like being around her at all. My instincts turned out to be correct. I'd later learn that she stole my varsity swimming sweats during the ten days I spent in the hospital.

I called my boyfriend and told him I felt like total crap. He invited me to spend the weekend with him at his parents' house. I eagerly accepted the invitation. Before he arrived to pick me up, I contacted a Christian Science practitioner. Practitioners are people gifted in healing and that dedicate their lives to helping others through prayer—listed by countries and states in the *Christian Science Journal*—that anyone can contact.

Despite the practitioner's support, my condition worsened during the night. My fever elevated until I felt confused and dizzy. An ugly rash appeared. My boyfriend's mom, high strung to begin with, said I might have bubonic plague. For the first time in my life, illness terrified me. Usually, my parents called a practitioner and whatever the problem was went away, so I never had a chance to become fearful. But now, fear of being permanently crippled or even dying raced through my mind.

I felt so isolated and alone. I was no longer surrounded by Christian Scientists — people like my parents who believed that Jesus came to demonstrate that material laws didn't have to control us, and that signs and wonders and healing — basically a recognition of our true, spiritual state of existence — could be experienced by any believer with a deep understanding of God. I felt vulnerable in this home where people feared illness and expected me to perish. I wasn't strong enough to fight off this heavy weight of their expectation of disaster, which church founder Mary Baker Eddy referred to as animal magnetism.

While all this commotion ensued, the phone rang. I had given the practitioner the family's phone number, so he could check on me. When he asked to speak with me, my boyfriend's father yelled at him and said that I would die if I wasn't taken to the hospital. Then he hung up on him. Fear seized me. I hadn't been allowed to speak to the practitioner. I had no one to comfort me except people who expected the worst. I started to lose hope. Guilt weighed heavy on me, too. I had caused chaos for my boyfriend and his family. If I survive, this will never happen again, I told myself.

An ambulance transported me to the hospital in Anderson. Upon my arrival, more chaos transpired. I had school insurance only the Clemson health center would accept. Because of our Christian Science background, my parents hadn't purchased any other medical coverage. Finally, the administrators admitted me and then the medical professionals asked me rapid-fire questions. Just let me lay down, I wanted to say. By now, I had a 105-degree fever and felt close to losing consciousness.

People talked about me as if I weren't even there. I caught little snippets of conversation. "She should have come in sooner." Then another voice. "I'm not sure what we can do." I felt too detached from my body to even care.

Someone wheeled me into a hospital room. The older woman in the bed beside me cried "Jesus, Lord, Mary, I can't take much more of this," repeatedly. It filled me with despair. Nurses came into the room constantly, even during the night. Just when I'd fall asleep, another person would come to take a blood sample or check my IV or take vital signs. My bed was on the side away from the window and I was separated from the other patient by a curtain. I didn't see the sunlight — even through a window — for ten long days.

My parents drove down from Ohio. My mother cried and cried. I felt so unhappy. I'd been healed of illness so many times when growing up I'd lost count of all the instances. I even got chicken pox my senior year in high school and felt completely fine two days later, even though it is considered to be a much more serious illness when contracted by a teen or adult. Maybe I hadn't been healed this time because I lacked faith. Maybe I hadn't been healed because I missed church whenever I was hungover. Maybe I hadn't been healed because I wasn't really listening to God anymore — I was listening to all the lures of the material world. Whatever the reason, my failure to apply Christian Science had caused horrible distress for my boyfriend and his family, a near breakdown for my mother, and I didn't even want to think about the hospital bill we'd be faced with.

Gradually, the antibiotics took effect and within a few days it was clear I would recover.

I left the hospital 20 pounds lighter. I still remember the day I was released. I stood up from the wheelchair and gazed around open-mouthed at maples, oaks, and elms, noticing how lush and green they looked. I paused to listen to the breeze rustle the leaves on the trees. Just inhaling a breath of the hot, humid summer air in South Carolina felt like heaven. I wasn't used to being trapped indoors, away from sunlight, away from trees. I smiled for the first time in days. My reawakening senses told me I was still alive. Immense joy and gratitude welled up inside my heart until I felt like I might burst. I wanted to turn a cartwheel, to shout with glee. Instead, I thanked God that I had survived.

Friends and teachers didn't recognize me because I looked gaunt and thin instead of strong and muscular — my summer tan had faded to a sick shade of pale yellow. I could only walk a few steps at a time.

Since I had missed too many classes, I withdrew from summer school. I was allowed to complete one course from my parent's house in Ohio, where I stayed after I was released. My parents didn't want me to return to Clemson. But I wanted to go back more than anything — I loved living in the Blue Ridge foothills and was really enjoying my geology studies.

I did return to Clemson. I raced in a sprint triathlon and won my age group category that October and completed my Geology B.S. degree two years later. But I turned my back on Christian Science.

CHAPTER FOUR

Cuzco, Peru -1996

*"If you aim to be something you are not, you will always fail.
Aim to be you."*
- Matt Haig's, *The Midnight Library*

I lived in Arequipa, Peru — known to many as the White City —
for two years in the 1990s, when I was still married to Sterling,
the father of my daughter Marion and my son Keith. No story
about my life would be complete without a snapshot of my time
in Peru. Although my marriage tottered on the brink of ruin,
that small sliver of time I spent living in Peru changed me.
Years later, I still find myself saying, "When I was in Peru…"

I'd tell people about experiences hiking, mountain biking,
and flying over the Andes in a helicopter with a group of
mining executives. I'd tell them about my failed attempt to
summit the 19,000-foot Misti volcano. I'd confess I'd had a
crush on my bodyguard and friend, José. I'd explain how

Sterling left me in Arequipa alone with two very small children with no security, no telephone, and no means of transportation. I fought hard to keep the three of us above water, leaning on a neighbor and people at the mining company office to help me acquire what we needed. I learned Spanish, hired a front gate guard and a bodyguard (since kidnappings and armed robberies were common), ordered a telephone service, and rented a car so we could buy groceries.

I'd explain how life moved slower—and how this initially drove me crazy but eventually led to a state of more tranquility. I'd tell them about my live-in servant named Fellie who cooked the most amazing meals and soon became a treasured friend.

In Peru, the walls I'd erected around myself gradually began to come down. I felt content with my small group of friends—Fellie, José, and two fellow expatriates, Jane and Holly. I'd been alone in the house with the kids most of the time until the relocation. Every night in Arequipa, Fellie and José ate dinner with Marion and Keith and I. On weekends, Sterling joined us.

I had a Spanish tutor. Month by month, my ability to speak the language evolved. At first, I could only talk to my new Peruvian friends about the weather but eventually we discussed politics, family issues, and relationships. In addition to many long, relaxed meals, I cycled almost every weekend with an International Club group, and rode with Fellie and José to the park with the kids. Marion and Keith loved to ride on the toy train or whirl around on the merry-go-round. Sometimes I'd take long walks with my friend Jane.

The country that at first had struck me as scary and intimidating turned out to be the place I experienced more connection and intimate friendship than I ever experienced in my life.

Our time in Peru ended abruptly. We were vacationing in Jamaica when Sterling's boss called and offered him another opportunity. A hostage situation in Lima, involving the MRTA terrorist group, had set us and other expatriates on edge. So we decided to accept the offer. The powers that be didn't even want me to go back to Peru. But I insisted. How could I not return to say goodbye to people and a country I loved so much? After a farewell week, I returned to the States feeling a deep sense of loss. But it was my chance to start over. And in the back of my mind I had this thought—maybe I'll get to live in another country again someday.

If it weren't for those years in Peru, I probably still would have clung to my belief that the U.S. is the only good place to live. Yes, there was terrorism in Peru. Yes, there is horrifying cartel violence in México. I would still rather live in either of these countries than the States. Americans have not typically been targets of these groups in either country. And at least school kids aren't getting slaughtered by shooters in either of these countries like they are in the U.S. In general, the lifestyle in my opinion is just higher quality outside the U.S.—calmer, kinder and less frenetic.

Since 1997, I have traveled to dozens of countries and can imagine living in many of them. In Peru, I learned that the fast and furious American pace didn't suit me at all. And so, 20 years later, I started living in México, experiencing another expatriate dream.

Below, I share a three-day hike I took on the Inca Trail in Peru, which was especially meaningful to me. The journey—where I connected with nature on a high level—was both meditative and spiritual. The rest of this chapter and the two that follow were written primarily from my 1996 perspective.

***

Jane and I had spent months planning to hike the Inca Trail. She lived in Arequipa also, her husband employed by Cyprus Mines Corporation. Five of us would fly to Cuzco, take a train to Ollantaytambo, and spend four days hiking to Machu Picchu. It would be a meditative journey, a physical challenge, an opportunity to enjoy the beauty and serenity of the natural world and learn more about the Incas. I couldn't wait to traverse the several unique ecosystems in the high Andes. It would be unforgettable, passing through the Gateway of the Sun and descending the stone stairs into Machu Picchu—the lost city of the Incas—far below.

It was still dark the next morning when our guide picked us up in a white van. We drove out of the Cuzco valley, emerging onto a plain, where a quilt of brown and pale green fields stretched over the earth. As dawn approached, the sky transformed from gray to purple to yellow-orange. Above the plains, a jagged row of mountainous teeth appeared. Julio pulled off the road so we could take photographs. The early morning air was crisp and the heads of purple flowers in the meadow bowed in the breeze. As we drove on, the front of mountains rose higher and higher before us until it became apparent that the flat road in front of us was about to make a tumultuous descent.

We stopped at a *mirador* that provided a view of the fertile valley thousands of feet below; the Sacred Valley of the Incas. The Urubamba River flowed like a tiny silver thread along the flanks of the plunging wall on which we stood; the sprinkling of Urubamba homes and buildings spread out below us appeared miniature. On the far side of the valley, agricultural terraces stepped up the slopes of the ice-capped Andean Mountain range.

Peruvian children tugged on our shirtsleeves. "Do you want to take picture?" they asked in English. Clad in brightly colored clothing, their complexions were scorched by the sun, their lips cracked and scabby. I photographed a young girl after handing her some *soles* and a package of cookies. She tucked her chin in toward her chest and looked up at me shyly for a moment before she ran over to show the package to a younger girl. As they laughed and tore open the package, I glimpsed their childlike spunk, which must have been smothered by daily struggles to survive. Gail asked another girl to take a picture of her and Barry. Afterwards, Gail handed *soles* to each of the children. I thought it was really kind of her, but her husband shook his head and said, "We can't help them all."

In a way, he was right. Even if you helped one child, there were thousands more lacking food, clothing, and shelter. But if every person said, "my time, money or food won't help anyway," more would perish. Changing the world is like the evolution of the landscape. Plates and continents move only millimeters per year, yet over geologic time, plains turn into mountains, super-continents split into smaller landmasses and equatorial jungles end up near the poles. It is the small choices each person makes that change the world for the better or the worse. You can't help them all, but you can help some.

The van descended the steep narrow switchbacks into the Sacred Valley, which contains Urubamba and a host of other villages, including Ollantaytambo, our destination.

The tourist train had already arrived by the time we reached Ollantaytambo, and clusters of hikers waited to begin the Inca Trail trek. Terracotta mountains were dusted with dagger-tipped agaves and prickly pear cactus. Spires of pink granite merged with the turquoise sky and in the distance Inca structures harmoniously nestled into an amphitheater of rock.

Julio instructed the porters and cooks who would carry our tents, sleeping bags, and food. *How will they hike wearing only rubber flip flops?* While we waited, women and children rushed up to us, waving tablecloths, dolls, walking sticks, and boxes of Chiclets in front of our eyes. We shook our heads. None of us wanted to carry any non-essential items.

Eight men and Nancy, our cook, tossed enormous loads on their backs. They would carry everything except our daypacks. In my pack was a long-sleeved shirt and rain parka, my camera, two liters of water and a bottle of my favorite *vino blanco*.

Our dark-skinned Quechua companions disappeared beneath enormous loads. Barely contained edges of cooking utensils, stools, tables, and toilet seats poked against the blue plastic sacks, which looked fit for Santa's sleigh, not for a man's shoulders. All of this for only five hikers and themselves. The complexity of sustaining a single man was immeasurable—so many of us occupying a space of earth, consuming, and making waste.

We crossed the suspended metal bridge spanning the Vilcanota River, which, in places, is called the Urubamba River. Julio explained that many villages and ruins along the trail were given Quechua names by Hiram Bingham, the Yale professor and explorer who rediscovered the lost city of Machu Picchu in 1911.

The trail led us higher and higher, until the roar of the river faded into the whisper of the afternoon breeze. *This is traveling. Not looking at geographical features from a bus window, but tasting mist on your lips, smelling fertile earth, and watching a new day open up like a chrysalis.*

At the higher altitudes, the Moya trees appeared, their tiny elongate leaves reminding me of the Arizona mesquite. Adorned with red pods, their branches dripped with Spanish moss.

The icy peak of Salcantay appeared on the horizon. As we continued our gradual ascent, more and more of its snowy flanks became visible; its pointed top pierced the cloudless blue sky.

After lunching in an open meadow, we trekked on to Huayllabamba (Place of Good Pasture), where we plopped down on a carpet of grass, removed our shoes, and soaked our feet in the icy Cusichaca Stream. The chilly water numbed my feet. I gasped and yanked them from the water, placing them on the grass, which felt like feathers between my toes. The afternoon breeze wafted a commingling scent of burning leaves and wet earth into my nostrils. I photographed my friends as they dipped their feet in the crystalline water, then focused my lens on a flock of wild turkeys.

We stepped inside a single-room mud and stone school building. I tried to imagine learning in this dark windowless room, with earthen floors and weathered wooden benches. There was no electricity and no sign of books, paper or writing utensils. *What are they taught?* I wondered.

The natural world offered so many possibilities for learning. I imagined teaching the children to identify trees, plants, flowers, and grasses. To close their eyes and name them through the touch of a fingertip, a scent.

Back on the trail, we hiked the last few miles to Tres Piedras, where we would camp for the night. Just outside Huayllabamba, villagers approached, laden with cold Cuzqueñas. At first, I thought it was a mirage. But soon the foamy beer was tickling my lips.

When we reached camp, our tents had already been set up in a neat little row, our duffel bags placed inside the doors. Moments later, I lay on my belly inside my tent, reading a novel. Just outside, two toddlers in shredded sweatpants chased each other and laughed. Their feet were bare, darkened by earth. As I thought of my two children, I felt a tug inside of me. Partially because I missed them, partially because my mind compared everything Marion and Keith had with everything so many Peruvian children lacked. *If only I brought some clothes my kids outgrew. Even one pair of shoes or jeans would be a precious gift to this boy and girl.*

A group of baby pigs, with pink and black mottled bodies and faces, roamed about. One stepped inside the tent, sniffing at my pack until I chased it out, vowing to keep the screen door zipped from then on. On more than one occasion, a little pig pawed at my door, clamoring to get inside.

Julio returned to our tents to recommend a nearby bathing spot — where crystal stream water rushed over a cement wall. Jane, Gail, and I were eager to check it out. Sticky with sweat, I was eager to drop my clothes in the tall grasses and step beneath the icy waterfall. The cold water made me shriek in pain and delight. My throat constricted along with my shoulder and back muscles, which were rudely awakened by the icy coldness. But at the same time, the chill energized me, made me feel suddenly alert. *I can solve complex equations, recite the theory of relativity, and enlighten my friends about my new plan to save the world.*

We walked back to the tent laughing and talking. I unzipped the tent and slipped on a pair of fuzzy wool socks before sprawling out prone on top of my sleeping bag with a notepad and pen. Crossing my ankles, I jotted down some of the day's experiences. I wrote until I realized it was getting dark. I should stop, I thought, as I flipped over to cardboard. I closed the note pad, peering at the pages I had filled.

What a day. Making this exhilarating trek through the Andes, my face caressed by cool, clean air, submerging my body in icy water, and allowing my thoughts and feelings to pour out from my heart and mind like a waterfall. My life feels so real. Away from my turbulent marriage and out here at one with nature, I feel at peace.

Hours later, Nancy served us hot bowls of spinach soup and each delicious spoonful warmed my insides. After I soaked up the last bit of soup with a piece of crusty bread, she placed a plate of chicken and vegetables in front of me.

Julio said we would climb Dead Woman's pass, known in Quechua as *Abra de Huarmi Wañusca*, the next morning. "From now on, I will refer to the *Abra de Huarmi Wañusca* pass as the tit," Julio said. Everyone laughed.

"You need to rest well tonight," he said. "It will take several hours to reach the summit and the ascent will be difficult."

I smiled. Climbing to the top of the 13,000-foot pass would be another challenge. One I couldn't wait to take on.

After dinner, I stepped out of the tent into the cold night air. The moonlight cast an ethereal glow across our camp and the surrounding mountains. Our camp was nestled in a V-shaped valley, which extended upward for miles toward Dead Woman's Pass. While the upper slopes of the mountains were illuminated by the rising moon, their flanks remained in shadow. Between the mountains, an array of stars sparkled in the midnight blue sky. As the moon rose higher and higher, silvery light trickled down the sides of the valleys, illuminating each jagged section. It was no wonder that the Incas worshiped the Pachamama, the earth mother, when they resided in a place of such awe-inspiring beauty. They had appreciated the earth's beauty and had never witnessed its tragic destruction the way I had.

I had stood aghast, visiting gouges in the earth where minerals had been taken like an organ from a body, the ground left open and bleeding. I had walked across asphalt parking lots where saguaros and prickly pear once thrived, shaken my head at the sight of homes and offices which blotted out once awe-inspiring mountain views. Mining companies and developers didn't care about trees and mountains, only bottom-line profits.

31

I may not be able to stop the destruction others inflict on the earth but maybe I can find ways to help the natural world.

An icy breeze sent me diving into my tent. I curled up in the warmth of my sleeping bag and fell asleep.

CHAPTER FIVE

Inca Trail, Peru – 1996

Julio's voice jerked me out of slumber. I rubbed sleep from my eyes and unzipped the door to receive a welcome cup of hot tea. We had an hour to wash and pack, Julio said. He pointed to a plastic basin of steaming hot water which had been placed beside the door. After a quick scrub bath, I dressed in layers, preparing for changes in altitude and temperature. I didn't realize how cold it was until my fingertips numbed. I dug my gloves out of my backpack and pulled them over my hands, relishing renewed sensation in my fingers.

After a porridge breakfast, we began the day's hike, climbing an endless staircase of stone steps through a dense cloud forest. In near obscurity, we stumbled through a forest of Polylepis trees, their thick twisted trunks red and white, their branches overflowing with foliage. Trunks and branches were decorated with strands of Spanish moss or Tarzan-style vines.

Tumbling waterfalls alongside the trail splashed my calves with icy water.

Whenever we emerged from the cloud forest, we caught glimpses of the ever-nearing pass above us. We crossed a grassy plateau, where wildflowers poked out their heads in yellows, purples and iridescent blue. Llamas munched on tall grasses, peered over at us with bulging eyes before they ran in circles, barking and nipping at each other's heels. Julio said two males were fighting over a female. I said some women have all the luck. He laughed.

As we began another steep ascent, the group's pace slowed. Disappointed to be pulled out of my meditative zone, I asked Julio if I could walk ahead and wait for everyone at the top of the pass. "*Porqué no*," he said, shrugging his stooped shoulders. Why not?

As I embarked on my solitary journey, I turned on my CD player. Hearing Al Jarreau's "Heaven and Earth" brought back memories of the amazing year I'd spent in Peru—my friendships with Fellie, José, Holly, and Jane. My relationship with our bodyguard, José, tipped dangerously on the edge of romance. But I was married and the tight bond we shared was too precious to muddle up with roller coaster emotions and hurt feelings. The two of us always had so much fun together. We'd drive places listening to ABBA, Phil Collins, and the Pet Shop Boys, talking and laughing like teenagers. In his company, I felt youthful and free.

He'd driven me all the way to Lima to meet Sterling for an office party and a shopping trip. Along our way to Lima, we stopped to walk along the beach in Camana. On our return trip, we stood out in a barchan dune field in the Atacama Desert in the middle of the night, gazing up at trillions of stars. We once mountain biked through the rugged mountains and rich green valleys of Colca Canyon, camping on the altiplano one night and then barely peddling into Chivay before dark the next. Peru had brought so many unexpected adventures.

I ascended the v-shaped valley, where expanses of prickly dry icchu grasses, in shades of lavender, sage, and emerald, dominated, then faded out at the higher altitudes, where slopes of naked granite projected into the sky.

My core temperature increased until I longed to peel off my Gore-Tex raincoat, my only protection from the icy high-altitude wind. I established a comfortable rhythm and before long, caught up with a group of young male hikers. Their accents suggested they were Australian or British. As I passed and said "hello," one of them engaged me in conversation. His hair was golden, disorderly curls accented his angular face. The color of tree bark, his eyes occasionally flashed to yellow when they connected with mine. Pleasantly disturbing.

He introduced himself as Nick before he asked my name and where I was from. As we walked, I answered his questions, told him about my life in Peru. Nick introduced me to his friends, Michael, and John. Michael's blond hair stood up in a tangled clump over his round, plump face; John's black shaggy beard contrasted sharply with his pale complexion.

"We're from Sydney," Nick said. "We're trekking in South America for a few months."

He told me about other hikes in Bolivia, Argentina, and Chile. He asked if I was hiking alone. I told him my companions were walking so slow, the ascent had become more of a chore than a delight. Walking briskly and feeling the endorphins flowing through my veins was more my style. His gaze wandered over me, eventually returning to meet mine. "How did you get in such good shape?" he asked.

Even in the cold, I thought my face might go up in flames. This guy was at least ten years younger than me, yet somehow, he found me attractive.

I told him about teaching fitness classes, the International Club mountain biking group, my love for swimming. I waited to hear the dreaded, "You look really good for your age." Instead, he said "That's impressive."

Wisps of clouds swirled around us. Soon we were enveloped by clouds. I felt as if we were entering a fantasy land. The fog would lift, and I would see Shangri-La, little hobbit homes far below, or a dragon with a fifty-foot wingspan soar across the sky.

The clouds spit out a fine mist and the wind intensified. I was sweating so profusely beneath the parka, my bra and T-shirt clung to my skin. I kept eyeing the summit, trudging upward only to learn that what I had thought was the top of the "tit" was not the summit at all.

When we reached the 4,200-meter high (13,779-foot high) pass, I was exhilarated to stand on top of the pinnacle, yet mourned the absence of a view. On a clear day, we would have been able to see hundreds of miles in every direction. Instead, we could barely see twenty feet in front of our noses.

A woman approached, offering us beers and sodas from a burlap bag she had slung over one shoulder. I handed her some *soles* in exchange for a Coca Cola. I popped off the lid and drank, allowing the sugar and caffeine to heighten my endorphin high. Nick photographed me standing on the pass amidst the tendrils of cloud. I snapped a photo of Nick and his friends before they picked up their backpacks. To reach Machu Picchu in two and a half days, they had to keep moving, Nick explained.

John and Michael offered a hurried goodbye, but Nick lingered for a moment. "It was nice to meet you," he said, extending his hand. I clasped it and a comforting warmth surged through me. When I let go of his hand and he turned away, a chill ran up my spine. Before long, all I could think about was the cold.

My friends were nowhere in sight. My neck muscles tightened and my teeth chattered. At that moment, a scene from *Flashdance* came to mind.

If Jennifer Beals can do it, so can I. I pulled my hands through the sleeves of my jacket and T-shirt and neatly slid my soaked bra and T-shirt out through my rain jacket sleeve. *Ah yes, much better.* My maneuver invoked a round of applause from a group of German tourists. I stood and bowed, waving my bra at them. When one of them produced a camera, I turned away. *This is too much of a good thing.*

By now, my friends were making their final steps to the top. Julio offered encouragement as Gail lifted reluctant feet, her toes tipped outward, her boots slipping in the scree. Her bellowing voice predominated over the howling wind. Clearly, she wasn't having fun.

Barry walked silently behind her, followed by Jane and Ken who trudged on persistently and without complaint.

Once they reached the summit, Ken clutched his knee. There was talk about which joints were creaking, what body part wasn't the way it used to be.

I tuned it all out to cherish the moment. *Beyond the clouds, there are layers of mountains all around me; I can feel their presence, their energy. I'll return to this place again someday. On a cloudless day, I will stand here on top of the world and see hundreds of miles across the horizon.*

I did return to Dead Woman's Pass. My Peru experience gave me the strength to leave my broken marriage after Sterling and I returned to the States in 1997. I met Chris Ferko in 1999 and we married outdoors the next year in Tucson with the Santa Catalina Mountains serving as a backdrop. In 2006, we traveled to Peru, visiting Lima, Arequipa, and Colca Canyon, before hiking the Inca Trail. We summited Dead Woman's Pass on a cloudless day and in every direction, we saw miles and miles of Andean peaks.

CHAPTER SIX

Inca Trail, Peru – 1996

We descended thousands of stone steps to reach Pacaymayu camp. My overtaxed leg muscles felt like pasta noodles after summiting Dead Woman's pass, so I cautiously placed my feet so as not to turn an ankle. Dialing 9-1-1 wasn't an option.

I sighed with relief when we reached camp. I snuggled up inside my sleeping bag, reading a Rosamunde Pilcher novel. Our tents were nestled in a cozy green valley, beneath a canopy of trees accented with yellow flowers, surrounded by tumbling waterfalls, which merged with the trickling waters of the Pacaymayu stream. The valley was rife with green and purple pampa grass. Low lying clouds lurked about, occasionally unveiling previously hidden views of a rocky cliff or a tumbling waterfall.

I peered outside occasionally, to absorb tidbits of scenery. Parakeets dipped as they flew from tree to tree, in brilliant blues and greens. The diversity of flora and fauna on the trail was amazing. Where else could you ascend and descend from desert to cloud forest to jungle to high mountain terrain and back again over the course of only 25 miles? I drifted into an exhausted sleep, awakening to find my cheek wedged inside my book. I pulled an alpaca sweater over my head and stepped out of the tent to see what the others were doing.

"There's a shower," said Gail. She pointed to a thatched hut on the other side of the Pacaymayu stream. I walked across the narrow dirt path to check out the building. Inside, I stepped across the cracked cement floor. I drew my arms across my chest and shivered as a chilly breeze whistled through the open upper walls. A squeaky handle in the shower stall released water the temperature of melted ice. In the absence of warm sunlight, I couldn't face the "jungle spa."

Jane and Gail appeared for dinner freshly groomed. Jane had pulled her waist-length hair back into a wet ponytail, which dripped as she slid into her chair. Gail's wavy dark hair was almost dry, her full lips accented with lip gloss. My skin still sticky from sweat, I wore a hat to hide my untidy hair.

I opened my bottle of Santa Rita and poured wine for my friends. The flow of alcohol brought out everyone's lingering insecurities. I mentioned an annoying digestive issue. Ken said his knees hurt and the narrow trails terrified him so much, he wasn't sure he ever wanted to hike the trail again.

I told him that I also feared heights. What I didn't say was that I intended to return to the trail. This adventure felt too incredible to only experience once.

Jane said she was too old to do this anymore but loved the luxury camping. With tents set up and tea and food beautifully prepared and waiting for us, it couldn't get much better, she said. We all agreed, and Julio seemed gratified that we appreciated his team's efforts. It was hardly roughing it, having bowls of hot stew and plates of warm bread placed in front of us, seated inside a warm tent, getting high on residual endorphins and Santa Rita.

The next morning, we devoured pancakes the size of small Frisbees, left Pacaymayu, and climbed steeply upward toward the second pass. We stopped along the way to study the Runcuraqay ruins, a half circle of stones which offered a view of the valley below. The site, believed to have been a *tambo*, or a way post for couriers following the trail to Machu Picchu, had sleeping areas and stabling facilities.

Near the summit, we picnicked in an open meadow. On the far side of the pass, the trail descended toward a valley where islands of green moss floated on a midnight blue lake. When the trail narrowed, Julio said we were traversing the true Inca Trail, where most of the stones were the original ones laid during Inca times.

The trail descended to the base of the access staircase to a second, larger Inca ruin, Sayacmarca (Town in a Steep Place), built on a promontory of rock overlooking the trail. The walls of Sayacmarca consisted of rounded boulders of various sizes which seemed to have been hastily assembled, their interstices a garden of moss and other vegetation.

Archaeologists have identified several styles of Inca stonework. The half circular Runcuraqay ruins we had visited that morning exhibited the Pirka or rustic style construction. Farming terraces, storehouses, and homes for the common people were usually built in this modality, using rough stones, cemented with small stones and mud mortar. The awe-inspiring Cyclopean construction is most prominent at the Saqsaywaman fortress, near Cuzco.

The Imperial Inca style had been reserved for sacred buildings and temples throughout the Inca Empire, comprised of trapezoidal granite blocks. So many unsolved secrets surround the Inca sites, the issue of construction being only one of them. How did they cut the rocks so precisely? How did they move boulders taller than four men, weighing literally tons, and then stack them neatly on top of each other like lightweight blocks of foam?

Below Sayacmarca, we followed the trail down to the valley floor, where tall spires of bamboo grew alongside golden marsh grasses. A forest of tangled trees obscured our views of the surrounding mountains. Eventually, we emerged onto a broad emerald plain,once a shallow lakebed according to Julio. The Andes Mountains had formed—and were continuing to evolve—as the Nazca Plate plunged under the South American Plate, heating and buckling the crust.

It is so incredible the way the earth preserves its past while continuing to move forward. There was enough of the landscape's past evident that geologists could reconstruct what had happened. Yet the landscape never stood still or had regrets; it just evolved and changed according to the rhythms and shifts of the earth. I longed to follow that model for my life. To not allow the past to swallow me. To not allow myself to get stuck in a rut. To let God guide me forward with a sense of trust.

On the far side of the plateau, the trail led us upward into an engulfing world of clouds before we trekked through an eight-meter-long tunnel, carved through a mountain of rock. The clouds receded by the time we reached the third pass. Curved walls of trapezoidal stone marked the Phuyupatamarca (Cloud-level Town) ruins, which lay on a hillside below.

Looking behind us to the south, the immense snowy summit of Salcantay rose like a volcanic island from an ocean of mountains. The descending sun cast an orange glow across its icy summit. In front of us, the lush green pinnacle of Machu Picchu Mountain reminded us that the next day, our journey would lead us into this sacred city.

The narrow trail spiraled and descended steeply toward the Wiñay Wayna (Forever Young) ruins. I leaned into the mountain, trembling with terror whenever my feet slid too close to the edge. The wall of foliage that masked the precipice wouldn't save me. If I slipped into its dark green arms, the leaves would merely give me "high fives" as I tumbled thousands of feet downward, leaving a grizzly imprint in the Urubamba River valley far below.

The Wiñay Wayna ruins nestle into an amphitheater-shaped valley, obscured by the visitor's center that offers restrooms, showers with blessed *agua caliente*, and a restaurant and bar. I made a beeline for the shower stall. Surrounded by walls of baby blue tile, I relished the warmth of the water, emerged feeling invigorated, my skin smelling of Ivory soap. I combed out my hair in front of the rusted mirror and then pulled on a clean tank top and pair of jeans.

Until dinner, the five of us drank *Cuzqueña* beer and played *Sapo* (Frog) outside on the lawn, taking turns trying to toss small stones into the wide-open mouth of a large metallic frog.

Our tents had been set up in a neat row along the ridge, overlooking Machu Picchu Mountain. In the morning, I awoke before dawn, sat on the grass outside my tent and watched the sky transform from gray into an array of pastel colors before blue sky appeared with the sun. Spirals of clouds hovered around Machu Picchu Mountain, cloaking it in an aura of mystery.

I was sad that we would soon leave this place. In two days, I would awaken in my Cuzco hotel, to the sound of car horns and shouting vendors. And instead of an ocean of mountains, my hotel window would reveal a sea of reddish-orange mission tile rooftops.

I never wanted to forget how it felt to be here. I loved this mountainous terrain in Peru more than anywhere else on earth. I never wanted to forget how this place brought me peace.

We traversed a narrow pathway overgrown with greenery until we stepped into the ruins of Wiñay Wayna. The rising sun illuminated the amphitheater of rock embedded in a lush emerald jungle. "Water sources such as springs, mountains and waterfalls were considered sacred by the Incas," Julio told us. He pointed to a waterfall which tumbled from rocky precipices above us. "These waters come from the melting snow of Salcantay."

The edges of the Wiñay Wayna ruins were slowly being consumed by jungle. Green, orange, and white lichen covered the rocks, causing them to crumble; yellow and pink wildflowers burst from the rocky interstices. Stony walls disappeared into forests of philodendron—their broad waxy leaves longer than my arms.

As we continued our journey to Machu Picchu, I imagined the Incas wouldn't be devastated by the fate of their city. They had built structures that embraced, rather than conquered, the surrounding landscape. If only the thousands of visitors could acquire and take home that vital connection to the earth. The Incas had set an example of how humans and nature could co-mingle. Each trapezoidal window framed a view of the surrounding landscape, each rocky prominence was carved to replicate the shape of a mountain, to utilize the angle of the sun, to point toward nearby mountains or cities.

The Incas believed in many Gods and sacrificed humans to appease them. Although polytheism is contradictory to my spiritual beliefs, I do share the Inca's golden rule approach to Pachamama or mother earth. They believed the earth bestowed many blessings on them and showed their respect to the mountains, rivers, rocks, sun and moon by erecting temples to honor them. Their structures all blended harmoniously into the hills and mountains.

"We're almost to the Gateway of the Sun," Jane said, interrupting my thoughts. "Are you OK?"

"Oh, yeah, fine," I said. The doorway of stony blocks undulated beyond my lens of tears. I quickly wiped my eyes with my shirt sleeve.

We stood on the threshold of Intipunku, the Gateway of the Sun, a trapezoidal doorway which provided our first view of Machu Picchu far below. We studied in awe the agricultural terraces, the city beyond with its grand plazas, stone buildings, water channels and temples, which lay before the two triangular spires of Huayna Picchu Mountain.

After more than three days of hiking, we would step into this ancient city more than 500 years old. We asked a passing tourist to take our picture as we stood together, our arms elevated and linked in triumph.

Once we reached the main entrance, Gail said, "Since we've all been here before, why don't we head to the restaurant, put up our feet, and drink some beer."

Everyone in our group liked her plan except me. I'd been here twice before on two family trips, but this wasn't the same. We hadn't come up on a bus—this had been a meditative journey—where every step had taken me closer to feeling in harmony with the earth, with myself. As Gail led the way toward the restaurant, I faltered. I couldn't waste the day chasing down Motrin with beer. I wanted to enjoy every precious moment here.

"I'd rather explore for a while first," I said. "I'll meet you back here in three hours, okay?" I left their surprised expressions behind and began my solo journey through the labyrinth of ruins.

Two major geologic faults, the Machu Picchu and the Huayna Picchu fault, caused a wedge-shaped block of earth to drop relative to the two peaks which now project as jagged pinnacles on either side of the city of Machu Picchu, which was constructed on this down-dropped block at 8,040 feet above sea level. The local geology couldn't have been more ideal for construction of this city, with the Machu Picchu fault providing a perennial spring for water and abundant fragmented granite for building.

I peered down at the Urubamba River, a meandering brown thread which circled the site on three sides, thousands of feet below. The mountain gods had protected Machu Picchu from the ravaging Spanish, who had conquered the Inca Empire, leaving the capital of Cuzco in ruins. More than a century would pass before Hiram Bingham rediscovered the "lost city of the Incas" in 1911.

In the river valley lay the rustic town of Aguas Calientes, from where, looking up, only towering cliffs of rocks were visible—as if this amazing city didn't even exist.

I'd stayed in a hotel in Aguas Calientes with Fellie, the children, and my mom when she had visited the previous year. We'd slept in beds with saggy mattresses, eaten some of the best *lomo saltado* (stir-fried strips of steak, onion, tomatoes, and potatoes) ever, and soaked in pea-green hot springs. My mom often mentions how special that trip to Peru was for her. She'd traveled alone—without my father—on this first trip to South America. It had been wonderful to see her relaxed and savoring unique experiences during the two weeks she visited. I've always enjoyed my mom's company and I felt especially close to her during those weeks.

I felt the energy of Machu Picchu flowing through my veins. A wisp of hair tickled my cheeks, and the cool morning air made my skin tingle and every fatigued muscle in my body sprang back to life. I skipped down a staircase of rocks, longing to shout with glee.

In the 1400's, the emperor Pachacuti Inca Yupanqui established Machu Picchu as a royal retreat. A stone wall separates the agricultural area from the urban area. The agricultural terraces that once produced maize and potatoes, divided into upper and lower sectors by the Inca Trail, are now covered with emerald green grass, conveniently manicured by grazing llamas and alpacas. The terraces minimized erosion that might have destroyed this city that literally rests at the edge of a precipice.

I leaped to the side as a group of llamas clomped past me on a narrow stone stairway. As I strolled through the *conjuntos*, or groups of walled buildings, my feet crunched over stone paths and stairways that led from one to the next, eventually taking me to the *kallanka*, or great hall, where festivals and ceremonies took place. Many buildings I passed had reconstructed thatched roofs and block walls of white granite in a *wayrona* style; three sides, with one of the longest sides open to the elements.

The entire city was harmoniously nestled into the landscape and surrounding mountains. Existing stone formations had been carved into floors and walls, shapes, and sculptures; water flowed through cisterns and stone channels, and temples hung along steep precipices.

Stones sometimes mimicked shapes of the surrounding mountains and strategically-placed temple windows offered spellbinding views. I stopped to revisit The Temple of the Sun, which served as a solar observatory, and the principal sundial, Intihuatana (Hitching post of the Sun), located at the highest point in Machu Picchu; used to track both time and date.

Historians have been unable to establish whether the residents of Machu Picchu died of hunger, succumbed to smallpox and other illnesses, or merely moved on. Mystery shrouded the city's fate, the way the wispy strands of cloud obscured the Huayna Picchu summit.

After crawling on my hands and knees with my nose nearly in the mud — terrified by the drop offs and slippery slopes — to the Huayna Picchu summit, I descended and stopped at my final destination. The sacred stone. People stood alongside this boulder more than 20 feet long that has been carved into the shape of a mountain, touching it, murmuring to it, crying. I waited until I was alone. As I brushed my hand over the rock, the rough texture of intermingled quartz and plagioclase crystals numbed my fingertips.

I've always loved the sensory experience of nature. It makes everything about living feel more real. More intense. Like the earth is flowing into me and I am flowing into the earth. We are one and the same. No longer confined to the walls of my own body, I become part of the planet, rotating on an axis, moving in an orbit around the sun. I feel like I am a part of something powerful, divine.

I closed my eyes and placed my cheek against the stone. The granite caressed my face like a splash of cool water. My prayer would be heard here, I knew. "Please give me strength," I whispered. "To walk away from my marriage. And start over. And give me a reason to return." I loved Peru. And I knew all my colorful experiences of living in this country would remain in my heart forever.

What I didn't know then was that my Inca trail journey had led me many steps closer to lasting love. The next time I returned to Peru it would be with Chris, the man now my husband, whom I have loved for more than 20 years.

CHAPTER SEVEN

San Carlos, México – March 2017

"We think we have understood everything. But we have not. We have used everything." – Thomas Berry, philosopher

Trump was elected President. The disappointing outcome threw me into a major depression that lasted for weeks. Headaches plagued me almost daily. Personal training clients continued to share stories of illness, age-related decline, death. It wasn't that I didn't empathize with them—I did—very deeply. But I found it painful to hear about their suffering when I felt helpless to do anything to alleviate it.

Sometimes I'd look out the window at the Santa Catalina Mountains and longingly remember my peaceful morning swims in the Caribbean Sea the previous year in Nicaragua, the joy of practicing yoga outdoors surrounded by trees. Peace and harmony seemed absent from my life. Even when I taught yoga, there was no peace to be found. Dropped weights crashed to the ground in the middle of savasana, vibrating the wooden floor. Fox News headlines flashed from the row of TVs in the gym, clearly visible through the room's windows.

Life in America was wearing me down. Yoga was supposed to help me control the path of my thoughts, but somehow it wasn't happening. I thought too often about illness, about my own recent decline in health. And I felt a sense of hopelessness and despair that I couldn't ease my clients' suffering or my own.

I wondered if I'd made a mistake moving away from Christian Science. One of the fundamental beliefs of this religion is that our true bodies are spiritual, not material, and that God created us free of discord of any kind. Is it too late to come back to it, I often asked myself. Other than attending an occasional church service or reading one of the publications here and there, I hadn't practiced Christian Science in more than 30 years. I sometimes prayed. But I only felt God's presence in rare instances, mostly when outdoors.

The drugs I'd been prescribed weren't reducing my migraines. A condition that had once been a nuisance had progressed to crippling.

At the beginning of 2017, I requested a two-month leave of absence from my job as a personal trainer and instructor. My husband was planning to retire soon, and we'd talked about living in another country. Maybe that would bring the fresh start that I needed. We considered Costa Rica and Panama but then decided before going that far away, we'd seek someplace closer.

My husband suggested San Carlos, México. We'd gone to San Carlos for scuba diving weekends, and we thought it might be worth checking out. An easy drive from Tucson, we'd be able to return to the U.S. to shop or visit family whenever we wanted.

During my leave of absence, I reserved a condo at the Pilar Condominiums on the outskirts of San Carlos. Chris drove down with me for a few days and then flew from Hermosillo back to Tucson. I stayed for ten more days.

The condo overlooked the El Soldado Estuary — a protected wildlife area overgrown with mangroves and rife with sea birds. Every morning, I'd awaken to watch the rising sun ignite the mirror of smooth water brilliant orange and see the jagged volcanic pinnacles shrouded by a salty haze. It was so peaceful. I'd hear only the chatter of the birds and the soft sigh of the sea.

Despite the cold temperatures, I swam in the sea daily. Those peaceful moments in the water reminded me of the weeks I'd spent the previous year on Big Corn Island, Nicaragua at a yoga teacher training, when each day had opened with a Caribbean Sea swim.

From the water and in the estuary mangroves, I saw herons and ibis, egrets, and frigate birds. The oyster catchers with their bright orange bills flapped their wings faster than any bird I've ever seen other than a hummingbird.

One morning, I saw dolphins in the distance from a stand-up paddleboard visitors Joy and Buzz let me borrow. Standing up above the water, the sunlight illuminated the underwater world clearly. I saw stingrays, hermit crabs, fiddler crabs, and fish. I even saw sea turtles I later learned were Olive Ridleys, the turtles that most often nest on San Carlos beaches.

I glided over the sea's smooth surface and noticed a boat full of tourists chasing the dolphins. I paddled furiously to get nearer. But it was worth it to get a closer view of those dark fins knifing through the water. I watched in awe as one jumped. Each time one surfaced for breath, a cloud of spray burst from its blowhole.

Two days before my return to Tucson, I took an afternoon walk to the estuary and spotted an injured seagull on the sand, wings splayed, supine. Maybe it just hurt a wing and needs to be turned over, so it can move better, I thought. I found a shell and used that to flip the bird over on his belly.

That's when I saw the mortal wound, bloody, revealing some of the bird's internal organs. It must have been attacked by another gull or a frigate bird. I'd seen some nasty fights among birds over fish in recent days.

Tears streamed down my face. I couldn't save him. I spoke to him instead. He looked so sad and vulnerable, expectant almost. As if he actually thought I could help. The best thing I could have done then was break his neck to end his suffering, but I couldn't bring myself to do it.

Maybe he doesn't want to die, I told myself. I knew I was lying to myself. How could this bird that has flown over water and buttes and seen the amazing El Soldado Estuary from high in the sky want to lie on that beach bleeding, dying, and knowing he would never fly again on this earth, that he would never catch another fish on this earth? All I could offer was a prayer that his spiritual being would travel on to a new place where he wouldn't suffer anymore.

The next morning before leaving San Carlos, I took a final walk on the beach. I knew what I'd find before I saw it. The mortally-wounded bird now lay dead in the sand, his feathers wet with seawater, his legs at an awkward angle, his eyes unseeing. The day before he'd been a struggling, vulnerable creature. Now he was a corpse. Where had his existence flown to, I wondered. Could it be to a place where one creature didn't feed on another, where pain signals from nerves didn't make one nearly lose one's mind?

CHAPTER EIGHT

March 2001 - Ambergris Caye, Belize

Chris and I married on March 3 — outdoors near Pusch Ridge in northwest Tucson — surrounded by our children, families, and friends. A minister named Jeff from a community church performed the ceremony. I'd finally met the man I belonged with, who understood me, who believed in me, who I trusted would be there for me in good times and bad times. Love and gratitude welled up inside of me as I thought about how much I looked forward to our life together.

We celebrated our first night married at the Westward Look Resort. We drank a glass of champagne in the high-ceilinged room before Chris unpinned the small wreath of ribbons and purple and blue flowers from my hair.

Three days later, we boarded a plane for our week-long honeymoon in Ambergris Caye, Belize.

More people drove golf carts than cars on the island. We rented a golf cart to explore one day. There was a small grocery store and some restaurants and shops in nearby San Pedro. In the rural areas, we saw many destroyed buildings and downed trees, casualties of Hurricane Keith, which had struck the previous year.

Our week in Belize fell short of romantic. The Exotic Caye resort wasn't as glamorous as it sounded. Our room had a kitchen and a small sitting area, but the sheets on the bed were scratchy and loud music at the nearby Green Iguana played until late into the night.

A group of Canadians—all friends—were also staying at the "resort" and planned to dive all week, but it had been so windy, they often called the dives. We dove along the reef near shore only twice.

Our big plan for the week was a scuba diving trip to the famous Blue Hole. The night before we boarded the boat, I lay awake half the night listening to the wind howl, sure our trip would be cancelled. But the boat captain was determined and after bouncing our way over waves (and landing with a resounding crash repeatedly) for two hours, our backs hurt but we had reached the Blue Hole.

The Blue Hole is a large sinkhole or collapse in a limestone cave system situated along Lighthouse Reef. The circular structure has a diameter of 984 feet and is 407 feet deep. It was likely formed during the last Ice Age when sea levels were lower than they are today. As temperatures warmed and many glaciers melted, sea levels rose and water flooded the caves, causing some of their roofs to collapse.

As our boat approached, the brilliant ultramarine water in the reef around us was shallow and crystal clear. Beyond the bow of the boat, I saw the ring of white reef and the almost midnight blue water in the circular center. It was awe-inspiring to approach this immense geologic structure that I had previously admired in photos.

Jacques Cousteau once declared the Blue Hole to be one of the top ten scuba diving sites in the world. I was soon to learn why.

I fidgeted and ground my teeth together as I geared up and checked Chris over before the dive. Both of us only have basic PADI certification, which essentially qualifies us to do dives 60 feet or shallower—not deeper-than-100-foot dives. I'd experienced nitrogen narcosis—a state of dizziness, intoxication, and/or confusion that can result from breathing compressed gases—at a depth of 80 feet on a San Pedro Island dive near San Carlos a few years earlier and wasn't sure I wanted to experience that again.

A deep dive where you hover around the bottom is reasonably safe. If you have buoyancy problems with the vest known as the buoyancy control device or BCD and end up on an out-of-control descent (which happens if you descend without enough air in your vest), the worst thing that can happen is that you crash land on your butt on the bottom. Since the Blue Hole bottom is more than 400 feet down, from a recreational diving perspective, it is a bottomless dive. Any diver that loses control and descends rapidly downward wouldn't be coming back up. That diver would end up what *Shadow Divers* author Robert Kurson referred to as a "creature feature"—a dead diver whose face became unrecognizable after being nibbled by fish.

That's not where I wanted to be. The divemaster gave us a detailed briefing. We would descend to about 110 feet, stay down for a very short while and then slowly ascend at no faster than one foot per second and hang out for a long decompression stop on a sandy bottom at 25 feet, where extra tanks would be left in case anyone ran out of air.

Pressure increases with depth. When air in your tank is compressed, you consume it faster. I can normally stay down for nearly an hour during a dive with a maximum depth less than 60 feet. The divemaster told us our total dive time—including our ten-minute decompression stop—would be less than 25 minutes.

Once we were given the go ahead, we descended slowly into the depths, the light fading out with every foot we traveled downward. We floated along the margins of the wall in deep blue darkness. The divemaster pointed out stalactites and stalagmites in some of the limestone crevices and underneath overhangs. I was unable to enjoy the experience. Dizziness and light-headedness overwhelmed me.

I glanced at my gauge. We were at 150 feet. *No wonder I feel like I'm about to black out. I shouldn't be down this deep.* I made a hand motion that I would ascend and level off. When I'd been at 80 feet in San Carlos, I'd gone up slowly a few feet until the lightheadedness passed and then gradually descended again, and my head had stayed clear.

Apparently, the divemaster didn't understand me because he approached and gripped both sides of my vest so I couldn't ascend. Panic seized me. And I fought to control my fear. This wasn't a light bit of nitrogen narcosis that felt like a beer buzz or laughing gas. This was a the-lights-are-about-to-go-out feeling. *What if I pass out?*

I needed to ascend but couldn't. I desperately called on God. *Please help me.* I didn't want my life to end like this—with me becoming one of those creature features and Chris having to make the return trip back to Ambergris Caye and eventually Tucson without me.

Fortunately, the deep dive time passed quickly. I silently thanked God when the divemaster released my vest and we all began our slow ascent. The lightheadedness and confusion rapidly dissipated. Warm gratitude welled up inside my chest. I knew I would make it safely to the surface. One young man had run out of air by the time we reached the sandy ledge for our decompression stop and had to suck air from one of the tanks left on the bottom.

After surfacing, we boated to Half Moon Caye Island for wall diving. Chris ran out of air quickly on the first dive, but it was amazing floating over the gentle waves while we waited for the other divers to come up. The water was so crystal clear. I saw colorful fish swimming below me. Nearby was the island—a lush jungle surrounded by snow-white sand. After landing and lunching at a picnic table, shaded by trees, we walked to the other side of the island through a tangled jungle and ascended a tower to see the nesting red-footed booby birds in the canopy of trees. Then we boated to the wall of reef around the island for our second dive. It was destined to be a dolphin-filled afternoon.

The bottom at Half Moon Caye wall was also essentially bottomless. We were instructed to cautiously descend to about 80 feet and then follow the contours of the wall. Life flourished on this pristine reef. Branching corals and waving plants in every color of the rainbow wowed me with every kick of my fins. The reef looked almost too brilliant to be real.

Just when I thought the dive couldn't get any better, three dolphins spiraled toward me. They playfully circled around me and then seemed to be playing a game with each other. After a minute or two, they disappeared into the depths. They were spinner dolphins, the divemaster later told me.

We sipped pineapple margaritas on the boat trip back to Ambergris Caye. Pleasantly buzzed, I leaped to my feet and shouted with joy when our dive boat was suddenly surrounded by hundreds of the spinner dolphins I'd seen earlier on our dive. A few dolphins jumped in our bow wake while others propelled themselves high into the air and turned somersaults all around the boat, putting on a performance.

That day, in addition to experiencing a minor but uncomfortable case of decompression sickness (from too many deep dives followed by alcohol consumption), I developed a serious and long-lasting case of dolphin fever.

CHAPTER NINE

San Carlos, México – May–August 2017

Two days before I planned to return to work, my boss said she preferred that I didn't come back. My clients had been working with other trainers. It would be best, she said, if I didn't interrupt their flow. She didn't want them to have to face another transition if I returned and then had to take leave again because I couldn't handle the workload, she said.

I felt a mixture of relief and sadness. I hadn't anticipated this happening and wasn't emotionally prepared for it. My heart weighed heavy hearing she had lost all confidence in me. It hurt not having the chance to say goodbye to my clients—many of whom I had trained for years and cared deeply about. But at the same time, I understood that it would be better for them to avoid disruption and sudden changes. I had lost confidence in myself. I wasn't sure I could provide what they needed anymore.

The good news was my schedule was wide open. I could flee back to México.

Chris took the news well. He encouraged me to spend more time in San Carlos. I can't imagine any husband in the world being more understanding than Chris. He has always made it clear that he wants me to do what is best for me.

His unwavering support and belief that I would eventually triumph enabled me to succeed at writing. I get frustrated easily and often wanted to give up. He's accustomed to persevering. When I tried for six years to get a book published, he kept saying maybe the next submission would yield a "yes" response. So, I forged on and eventually obtained a contract and in 2012 published my first book. Since then, I've published dozens of books, including two fitness books and many romance novels under the pseudonym Sabrina Devonshire. Maybe Chris's good traits are rubbing off on me.

We booked a condo at Bahía Delfín — a condo complex adjacent to the Pilar complex where I'd stayed in March — for the whole month of July. We bought that very same condo one month later.

One of those first days as a new owner, I walked down to the estuary while light rain fell. The mountains were shrouded with clouds and cool air kissed my face, smelling of earth and rain and salty sea. I saw several herons and a flock of white terns. A group of tiny sandpipers flew toward me in unison and then did a jerky about-face before heading in the opposite direction. Most of the birds had gathered out on a sand bar, which often appears in the middle of the estuary at low tide.

I saw several large Green Crabs in the water, probably four inches wide. Even so, they were smaller than the snow-white and startlingly large Ghost Crabs I'd seen in Nicaragua. I spotted numerous hermit crabs dragging their adopted shell homes along the sandy bottom. With no dogs and humans around, the estuary teemed with life. I had to be silent and aware to take it all in, though. I felt very at peace. I was present, really living while raindrops dampened my skin. I watched a tern fly across the water and then another one joined him, emitting a high-pitched, shrieking call. A heron issued some low-pitched squawks. A jumping fish splashed into the water.

I could have stayed there for hours but eventually, I strolled back to the condo. Most home and condo sales in México include the contents — furniture, bedding, wall art, dishes, pans. I had told the realtor that if the owners wanted the large dorado (fish) hanging on the wall — they could keep it. I didn't much care for it and figured it might have been a prize catch the owners would want to keep. It was gone when we came to the condo for the first time. Chris asked about it and I told him I'd said the owners could keep it. It was the only thing in the condo he had really wanted, he said. But he hadn't shared that wish with me. Until now.

I said I could ask the realtors what had become of the fish. He said no, it wasn't important. But I know him. Sometimes he'll say something doesn't matter when it does, perhaps because he doesn't want to upset me or has begun to think his needs aren't important since he's been worried about me.

My long stints away from home, chronic migraines, and sudden unemployment, compounded by the unplanned expense of buying this condo had weakened the seams of our marriage. I wondered sometimes — did Chris still want to be with me, or had I become another obligation?

So many couples drift apart and divorce. I'd divorced before. But I wanted more than anything for this marriage to work. I couldn't picture myself with anyone except Chris. I loved him as much as I was capable of loving another person — living the way I was in survival mode. Every day was a desperate struggle to avoid a migraine. I wanted so much to elevate that "love" to a different plane where it was more about making his life better and less about grappling for a few hours of freedom from pain.

I decided to paddle around on our new kayak. I spotted a sea turtle popping his head up for air. Out on the water, I thought about how much I loved Chris. And I decided I would try to get the mounted dorado back. It would mean I would have to step out of my comfort zone, but how often did Chris do that for me? Pretty much daily.

Once I got back inside, I called the real estate office and asked Sergio if he knew what had become of the dorado. The previous owner had donated it to the El Mar dive shop, he said, but I could call about it if I wanted to. Since my husband had returned to Tucson with the car, my friend Allison drove me there to explain the situation. The owner, Feliza, hadn't figured out where to put the stuffed fish and seemed happy to return it.

We could barely squeeze the four-foot-long fish into Allison's jeep but an hour later, the dorado was back hanging on our condo wall. When I called and told my husband that I had succeeded in getting him back, I was thrilled to hear his voice rise with enthusiasm. This simple gesture had made him happy. To me, it symbolized a new chapter of my life — not only a chapter where I would swim in the sea daily, practice yoga more often, and heal my body, but one that would transform me into a more caring person. Chris named the blue and yellow fish Ace and he's still hanging on our bedroom wall.

One evening at sunset, I walked alone on the beach toward the El Soldado Estuary. In shallow water, I spotted a large sand dollar. I reached down to pluck the plate-sized treasure from the water, amazed at its nearly pristine condition. It was more than three inches in diameter. Two young Mexican girls, probably around five and seven years old, splashed in the water nearby. They stopped running and gazed at me. Speaking in Spanish, I asked them if they wanted to look at it. They ran over so fast, they splashed water everywhere.

They touched and admired the sand dollar, remarking on how big it was. Even though I had planned to keep it, I asked them if they would like to have it. They eagerly burst out with "Sí" at the same time.

They walked away with my sea treasure, but I walked away feeling a sense of joy and elation I hadn't experienced in a long time. This simple meaningful connection with the local people and this act of giving made me feel like I could fly.

Days passed and I realized I'd never been this content. I no longer needed to leave town or acquire another material possession to feel happy. A swim in the sea, a walk on the beach, some hours writing, or quality time with my husband were all I needed.

The negative emotions that had constantly plagued me receded to the fringes of my consciousness. *It isn't too late to start over. It isn't too late to change. I belong here. This is where I'm supposed to be. Here, I will become a different woman, the one God meant for me to be.*

CHAPTER TEN

Oro Valley, Arizona and Worthington, Ohio – 2008-2015

In 2008, I joined the Ford Aquatics Masters swimming team. My major motivation for embarking on challenging, structured training workouts was emotional release. My father had just been diagnosed with stage 4 bladder cancer. I couldn't wrap my head around it. He'd experienced excellent health most of his life. Now, all at once, he was debilitated.

Once my father received the cancer diagnosis and we pressured him into getting medical treatment, he stopped listening to the classical and opera music he'd always loved, he stopped mowing the lawn, and he stopped working out at the Sawmill Athletic Club. It was horrifying to witness this change. I longed for a return to our normal disagreements and his irritating lectures. He had been a Christian Scientist most of his life and I still wonder if pushing him onto this path led him to give up.

My brother and I weren't practicing Christian Science. The thought of not seeking medical treatment in an emergency terrified me ever since I'd come so close to dying in South Carolina.

Some people had what it took to experience healing, I thought. Discipline and ethical, spiritual living were requisite. I lived what I considered an ethically-based and honest life, but I wasn't particularly disciplined or spiritual. My father had some hang-ups, but he never failed to study and pray for us every morning. Until recently, he hadn't seen a doctor or been in a hospital in decades. He'd relied totally on God for his care and had experienced excellent health most of his life.

Despite this medical emergency at age 71, what he trusted was God. He found hospitals scary and unfamiliar. He didn't believe disease was the true state of anyone's being. He didn't believe in matter or solid objects at all. He believed every person, creature, tree and plant and every other aspect of the universe was completely spiritual. He believed an illness or abnormal growth would disappear if a person saw how God created him or her—in a state of flawless harmony—as a spiritual, rather than a material being.

Christian Science founder and author of *Science and Health with Key to the Scriptures*, Mary Baker Eddy, wrote, "Disease is an image of thought externalized." Jesus healed suffering people as a daily part of his ministry and Eddy also said, "these mighty works are not supernatural, but supremely natural." She believed they are a sign that God is with us and ever available to erase suffering.

Eddy also had a deep love for nature. She healed injured birds as a youth and often described the beauty of the natural world in her writings. In her book, *Miscellaneous Writings*, she described flowers as the "smiles of God." She loved flowers so much that children in her Concord, New Hampshire neighborhood often referred to her as "the flower lady."

Since the religion's beginning in 1879, thousands of people of faith have overcome illnesses ranging from common colds to heart disease and cancer. These healings can be read about in *Science and Health, Mary Baker Eddy: Christian Healer*, the *Christian Science Journal*, and the *Christian Science Sentinel*.

Unfortunately, during the time of my father's illness, my faith in God was feeble. Some nights I'd sleep blissfully, temporarily forgetting, and wake up in the morning and think to myself something was terribly wrong before it would all come back. *My dad's got cancer.* Instead of praying for him the way I would have now, I felt overwhelmed with despair and rushed off to drown my feelings with another hard swim.

I flew to Ohio on and off throughout that summer. When in Tucson, I became a regular at 6 AM Masters workouts. I had stayed fit teaching classes and occasionally swam for fun, but it had been years since I'd pushed myself in the pool. I experienced a full spectrum of emotions when I swam — anger, sorrow, frustration, despair. I fought my way through these negative, raw emotions. When I exited the water at the end of a workout, a serene calm prevailed.

My Masters swimming journey turned tumultuous. Looking back, I wonder if the heavy weight of negativity I carried during that sorrowful time of my father's illness attracted some of these toxic experiences.

My most memorable Masters experience was racing in Summer Long Course Nationals in Portland in 2008. All the races took place in an Olympic-size, 50-meter pool. Despite my father's illness, I wanted to go. I longed for a change of scenery and a chance to get my mind off of things.

I went without expectations of any specific results and ended up placing second in the 45-49 age group in the 100- and

200-meter breaststroke and third in the 50-meter distance. What made the weekend even more thrilling was that the summer Olympics in Beijing were happening at the same time. I'd turn on the TV after my races to watch Ryan Lochte, Michael Phelps, Rebecca Soni, and Matt Grevers race. One night after the meet, we watched Dara Torres swim to a silver medal in the 50-meter freestyle. She was over 40, which made it super inspiring for Masters swimmers ticking up in years, yet still lured by the thrill of competition.

After my meet when I returned to Ohio and my mom and I took my dad in for another follow-up, his cancer doctor said he was too weak for chemotherapy and that he wouldn't live to see Christmas. My father — once broad-shouldered and strong, trembled in pain, and probably anxiety, overhearing his fate discussed as if he weren't even there.

Tears sprang to my eyes. I had encouraged my father to make this choice — to have a surgeon cut him open, remove his bladder so his urine had to be collected in an ostomy bag, and then a few months later, offer him a death sentence. I am not denying the dedication and many successes achieved by medical professionals. One of my condo complex neighbors had the same kind of cancer and is recovering. His faith in medical treatment supported his recovery. But lack of faith in any kind of treatment can make a person give up hope.

Whether my dad would have survived or not had we encouraged him to rely on his faith in many ways is a moot point. We'd urged my father away from what he trusted, and left him feeling hopeless and lost. I will always regret that this happened.

My father died on November 1. I still remember resenting the clear blue sky, asking God how the weather could be so beautiful on the day when my father had left the earth, when

I'd never see him again in this plane of existence. Yes, we'd always had a difficult relationship. I still felt broken.

Unsure how to cope with this overflowing well of sadness, I shunned prayer or quiet moments of reflection. Instead, I returned to work immediately. Competed in a meet in Phoenix. Trained in the water harder than ever. Downed glasses of wine at night.

Instead of allowing space for grieving after my father's death or feeling gratitude that he was in God's loving arms now, I'd buried my emotions. As a result, I descended into a perpetual state of anger, frustration, and dissatisfaction. I didn't want to be the dark storm cloud, the person no one wanted to be around. But I felt helpless to change this negative perturbation of my state of mind.

I trained in a lane full of long-time friends. I wasn't part of their clan. I felt like an outsider but felt too dead inside to even care. One day, I was leading a kick set. Apparently, I left five seconds late. One woman threw her fins across the deck and screamed at me before launching herself out of the pool. I waited for our coach to tell her to calm down. He did nothing. I had no option but to listen to her rant until the next repeat. This isn't fun anymore, I told myself. But I kept practicing anyway.

At a fall season meet, my coach asked me to swim the 100 fly as part of a 400 medley relay (all four competitive strokes are swum with the first swimmer doing back, the second, breast, the third, butterfly and the last, freestyle). The water and air were chilly, and I'd already swum a 200 Individual Medley or IM (which includes a 50 fly, 50 back, 50 breast, and a 50 free), as well as a 100 fly and a 50 fly. I told him I didn't think my shoulder could handle that. He kept pressuring me. I swam the leg to keep an elderly teammate from having to do it. And promptly tore my rotator cuff. After that, I quit the Ford

Aquatics team and embarked on six months of physical therapy. I resented that incident and the individual I held responsible for it for years.

Now, I ask myself if the injury ever would have happened if I hadn't been expecting it. I'm in such a different head space today. I injured my shoulder again at the Short Course State meet in 2022 (I was unable to sleep or lift the arm or get a shirt on for several hours) and instead of months of rehab, I called a Christian Science practitioner and raced again the next day without further consequence.

Blaming people after the fact only prolongs the suffering. Writing about an incident helps me release the anger. Praying about it and separating the person from the perceived wrong helps the most. Always now, I make an effort to forgive people.

Once my shoulder rehab ended, I joined the Flying Fish Masters team at the Oro Valley Aquatics Center. I enjoyed the company of the other swimmers, and the pool was just minutes from our house.

I also sometimes trained and raced with the SaddleBrooke Swim Club where I'd been graciously invited to swim since I worked at the fitness center in this active adult community. It was a joy and inspiration to swim with this group of enthusiastic senior swimmers. I embarrassed myself one Saturday morning when a sudden painful calf cramp incited me to yelp very loudly. A woman on the nearby pickleball courts called the police and an officer rushed to the scene to find the youngest participant in the swimming group in the hottub receiving a leg massage from a fellow swimmer.

I traveled to Omaha, Nebraska for Masters Nationals in 2012 with an expectation of becoming a national Masters champion in the pool where the Olympic Trials had been held days earlier. It was thrilling to walk from the Hilton across the glass corridor to the pool that had been constructed in the convention center — just like I'd seen Michael Phelps and Katie Ledecky do on TV earlier that week. I would finally have my chance to touch the stars.

I was seeded first in my age group in two of my breaststroke events. Instead of winning a national title, I lost my 100-meter breaststroke race in the final few meters — apparently because of an over taper — during a taper, an athlete decreases training and daily activity to race in a more rested state. Meters from the finish near the backstroke flags, I had virtually nothing left. I ended up placing third. I was so distressed about this failure, I found it difficult to approach my other races with a positive attitude. I finished a disappointing second and third in my other breaststroke events.

Falling short of my goal gave me flashbacks to high school, when seven or eight times I'd swum the same time in the 100-yard breaststroke, missing the Junior Olympic qualifying time by less than two tenths of a second. I hadn't achieved my goals then and once again, I had missed the mark.

I flew home feeling demoralized. The competitive swimming I once loved had become a source of misery.

And yet, I swam and raced for four more years. Swimming had always been my lifeline. Even though in high school, I'd suffered some disappointments, I'd preferred being a second-rate swimmer over not swimming at all. For so many years, my anchor had been swimming. I didn't know what else to do to keep my head above water in life.

I don't know now why I let my emotions get so out of control — why I let winning become such an obsession. As a Masters swimmer, I wasn't training for the Olympics or letting down a sponsor — all this mental chaos was tied up in personal ego and thinking I had to prove somehow I was acceptable and successful. A time on the clock or a first-place medal was never going to accomplish that for me. I could have decided at any time that I was enough because I was out there participating and God created me. And I could have listened to what God had to say to me instead of mindlessly rushing forward like I had a football helmet on and was putting my head down and trying to plow through a line of two hundred pound men. But I wasn't ready to do that just yet.

Our coaches took vacation breaks every summer before the Masters state championship and nationals event. Since this halt in training leading up to our major competitions sapped morale for some swimmers, including me, some of us emailed the board in the summer of 2015, requesting the timing of this leave be changed.

I attended what was to be the last morning practice before this break. One coach experienced manic mood swings. Suddenly, the coach flew into a rage. He ranted on and on. He said that our team was not a competitive team and that practices were for fitness only and we were conspiring to ruin his life. I shook and trembled. *How could this be happening? We're paying for these workouts. Why is he screaming at us?*

Apparently, wanting to achieve a goal as a Masters swimmer made me and my other competitive teammates insensitive jerks. Even if that didn't make sense, I internalized the coach's rant. Something always seemed to impede me achieving my swimming goals. It felt useless to keep trying. I didn't have to ask myself if swimming was fun anymore. I hated it. I couldn't wait to get out of the water and go home.

The Dolphins of the Desert team—led by Jeff Commings and Geoff Glaser—agreed to host our workouts leading up to the championships. My husband and I had airline tickets and hotel reservations for Summer Nationals, so we went as planned. Despite my gratitude to Jeff and Geoff, my enthusiasm for racing had been decimated. After that week leading up to 2015 Summer Nationals, I quit the team.

I didn't attend another Masters workout again until 2021 when I trained with a Solana Beach team while vacationing. Thankfully, I also enjoyed Masters workouts with teams in South Lake Tahoe and Albuquerque in 2022 where coaches and swimmers alike were warm and welcoming.

CHAPTER ELEVEN

Big Corn Island, Nicaragua – May 2016

Seeking to fill the void left behind after my Masters swimming debacle, I enrolled in a three week, 200-hour Ashtanga yoga teacher training. Most people take yoga teacher trainings or YTTS through their local yoga studios. I chose to travel to Big Corn Island, Nicaragua instead. Why take a series of weekend courses in Tucson when I could go to an exotic destination, immerse myself in the practice and learn about myself?

People asked me, why Nicaragua? Why not some off-the-beaten-path resort in the U.S. or even Costa Rica? Truth be told, I loved the idea of living on an island and being surrounded by water. People compared Big Corn Island to Gilligan's Island — a deserted island from a popular 1960's TV show where the Skipper, First Mate, and five passengers on board the *SS Minnow* were marooned after a storm.

Travelocity reports indicated few people lived on the island, there wasn't a single high rise, and it was mostly a wild tangle of jungle surrounded by the idyllic blue Caribbean Sea. Even though I had very little open water experience, being able to swim in the sea wildly appealed to me.

Three weeks of swimming on the island might rekindle my love for the water. The teacher training would allow me to practice savoring the present moment instead of constantly looking ahead to a future where I would buy some new thing or achieve some all-important goal.

And just maybe it would help heal my mind and my body. Migraines seemed like a runaway train in my life now, increasingly limiting my work and social life. I no longer was sure I had any power to stop them. I hoped at the training, I would learn some tools to help me move in a more favorable direction, to gain more power over my thoughts.

I flew from Tucson to Houston to Managua and then boarded a small plane to Big Corn Island. With no functioning AC on board, I landed with drenched clothes adhered to my skin, physically and emotionally exhausted from the journey.

Outside while waiting for a taxi, I learned two more people were going to the Paraiso Resort along with Kayla who I'd met on the plane. All four of us crammed into a tiny Suzuki sedan. The 20-something guy sat in the front while I crammed into the backseat beside the other two women, our sweaty feet and arms bouncing against each other during the drive.

The car wasn't a degree cooler than the plane. It had to be close to 100 degrees and 100 percent humidity. My thighs stuck to the seat, my drenched hair lay plastered to my cheeks. I tried to breathe deep and imagine the sea. *I'll check into my room and rush down to the water.*

After checking in, I walked across a grassy lawn lined with coconut palms to room number 8, a red-painted cement structure with a thatched roof. I stepped into my room and my mouth fell open in shock. Dark curtains blocked most of the light from the two small windows. It took a moment for my eyes to adjust to the dim light. Dark tile floors, a saggy mattress resting on a slab of cement, and a small grungy bathroom greeted me.

People who live in fancy homes in Oro Valley don't stay in places like this, I told myself. Maybe I'd made a horrible mistake. The weather was sweltering, and all our sessions would be in an outdoor yoga space or *shala*. For three weeks, I would have to sleep in this dump. I looked up and saw a line of fire ants on the ceiling. They must have been feasting on the wood up there for a while because a pile of shavings sat on top of the headboard. *Fantastic.*

I dropped my suitcase on the floor in disgust. At least there was an armoire to stow my clothes and a small desk I could use to study. When my gaze landed on the wall AC unit above the desk, I grabbed the remote, pushed the on button and gasped with relief as cool air poured out of the vent. The cool air felt amazing but what I really wanted to do was submerge my weary, overheated body in the sea.

As I rifled through my luggage for a swimsuit, someone knocked at the door. *Can't I have a minute of peace?* I opened the door and a woman who introduced herself as Ildica said there would be a meeting of all the yoga training participants in ten minutes. Panic struck. I knew I'd get a migraine if I didn't get some down time for self-care. I wanted to scream, "Are you kidding me?" How could they expect me to do this now?

I'd been traveling all day. Drenched in sweat, I smelled sour and probably had bad breath. Not to mention the mental and physical exhaustion. I'd spent the whole day in crowded, noisy places. What I wanted, what I needed was a swim—my typical solution to any problem—at least until recently. I grumbled something unpleasant to her and slammed the door shut.

I walked from my room to the outdoor *shala*—a broad expanse of smooth wooden floor raised several feet above the ground with open walls and covered with a thatched roof. It was surrounded by enormous broad-leafed trees, including a mango tree, which routinely dropped fruit into the tangle of plants below.

I introduced myself to the two yoga students in our group that I hadn't yet met—Melissa and Ashley, along with our lead instructor, Lucas, and the assistant instructor, Chelsea. I sat slumped over, feeling anxious and out of sorts—the early signs of a migraine. To be honest I don't even remember much of what was said. I really didn't care. I'm like that. If I am propelled into a state of total imbalance, my mind stops functioning and I'm not able to absorb anything.

It would be getting dark soon, I kept thinking. Then I wouldn't be able to swim at all. Why couldn't this stupid meeting just end?

After more than two hours had passed, we were dismissed. The others were talking about showers and dinner, but I had no interest in either. I sprinted back to my room, slipped into my swimsuit, and dashed out the door.

I raced down the conch-lined path, past dozens of coconut palms and crossed the road and there it was. The sea. The water looked smooth and faintly pink under the evening sky. Remnants of two sunken wrecks poked out from the water. I walked across the road. Piles of volcanic boulders separated the road from the narrow stretch of beach. Two small fishing boats sat partially buried in the sand.

Finding a spot free of reef rocks, I waded into the water. Happy chemicals raced through my veins for the first time that day. I'd anticipated meeting the Caribbean Sea for hours, days even. Our meeting had been delayed but not thwarted. I swam a couple hundred yards away from shore. The sea cooled and caressed my body, melting away the exhaustion and anxiety of the day. I rolled over onto my back, floating in the salty water, slowly kicking my legs. Above me, a purple sky and a slice of moon told me the day was coming to an end.

On shore, I saw no one—only an endless stretch of sea grapes and coconut palms. I released a long sigh, tasting the salt on my lips. What a blissful end to a chaotic day. Balance had returned to my being. My mind was alert and clear again. Every morning we'd start sessions at 7 AM. But I knew at 5 AM every morning, I'd swim in this amazing sea.

CHAPTER TWELVE

San Carlos, México – October-November 2017

Chris prefers gym workouts over sea swimming and beach walks. Occasionally, I drop in for Latin dance classes at the Athleticlub. I enjoy the rhythm of the Latin music and the expressive dance movements even though the music is so ear-piercing I have to stuff tissue in my ears to tolerate it.

But it's hard to drag myself to the gym when the Sea of Cortez, just steps from my door, calls me in a different direction, the one my heart wants to go. My beach workout can be sun salutations in the sand, an hour swim with intermittent rest to play with the dolphins, or a kayak journey to a nearby island or the estuary.

Always, first, I want to swim. A day without immersing myself in salt water feels like a day wasted, an opportunity missed.

The sea beckons me when I've been away from it— however briefly. Spotting blue-green water after driving through barren desert is especially startling. My heart rate elevates and my fingertips tingle. I feel compelled to stop the car, rush to the beach, and plunge into the water's blue depths.

Driving from Guaymas to Miramar, a right turn at the BestGas station leads me down a windy road surrounded by tall trees and tangling brush. I first spot an estuary and all at once am mesmerized by coastline, islands, and brilliant turquoise water. Driving east from San Carlos, when I drive past the Malecón — an esplanade alongside the sea — the broad curve of the bay appears. I will myself to keep my eyes on the road. *No. Don't look to see if the water's calm. Don't look for the dolphins.* It's hard to describe the magnetic pull I feel toward the water. Maybe I'm a land dolphin descendent, unsure whether dry or wet is natural for me.

One Saturday, when the water was crystal clear near the estuary, a dolphin glided underneath me. I glimpsed the broad expanse of his back and his two-pronged tail known as the fluke. I watched the graceful creature propel himself through the water. I saw a mother and youth swimming together and also dolphins swimming around that appeared to be feeding or playing. One dolphin initiated a hide-and-seek game with me. It would surface with its fin and then duck down and the next thing I knew she or he would be behind me. I couldn't help laughing. Being near them was so uplifting and fun.

Minutes later, a dolphin accelerated very fast about twenty feet away, creating a huge wake of water. It zoomed through the water like a rocket. The three fins and tail of a dolphin allow it to quickly swerve and maneuver.

I gasped when two dolphins started up a tail-smacking game. Water splashed everywhere. The game turned rough. Hide and seek was fun but getting rammed by a dolphin or tail slapped could be a bone-breaking experience for a fragile creature like me. Maybe this was a subtle warning — that they were moving slowly around me for now, but they could be much rougher if they wanted to be. Maybe they didn't want me to linger?

I was so close to these highly intelligent creatures. I longed to communicate with them, but couldn't. We'd have to learn to read each other by spending more time together, I thought. At that moment, I felt like I was being asked to hit the road.

I swam back to the beach in front of my condo. Back inside, I surfed the internet, reading about dolphin behavior. In the U.S. and some other countries, it's illegal to swim with wild dolphins because marine life protection agencies consider it harassment. Other websites suggested short interactions of a few minutes so as not to disrupt their routine too much. I loved and admired the dolphins and didn't want to interfere with their feeding, sleeping, nursing, and, well, sex. I hoped they perceived me as a friend rather than a pest.

CHAPTER THIRTEEN

San Carlos, México – August-October 2017

I gazed through my goggles and olive-green water. Another algal bloom. Changing temperatures and weather, agricultural runoff, and other contaminants can cause the algae to proliferate. I didn't enjoy murky water swims.

Thoughts linger in the back of my mind about what might be swimming nearby that I can't see, that might strike without warning. Suddenly, a dark shape shot by beneath me. I glanced toward shore. When I spotted one, two and then three dorsal fins around me, I sighed with relief. Just my new dolphin friends.

One dolphin swam just inches away from me, releasing a high-pitched squeak. Dolphins were in front of me and behind me and underneath me, gliding with such precision and control. And then they disappeared as suddenly as they had appeared. They'd checked me out. I'd disrupted their routine—

briefly. And now they probably wanted to move on to more important activities like catching fish.

Maybe they, like me, were uneasy, wondering if I could be trusted. They must have wondered what drew me into their environment when humans moved so awkwardly in water. Dolphins must know they don't belong on land and want to avoid it. Their lives revolve around survival. Swimming for exercise probably isn't something a dolphin can wrap his or her head around.

The humid heat melted away into fall. The changing season brought the return of many migrating birds. One night, Chris and I sat out on the wall above the beach while a layer of clouds hung over the ocean, bathing it in eerie white light. It must have made the fish more visible because more birds than I'd ever seen before hovered over the water and then dove for fish. Pelicans, gulls, terns, and American oyster catchers. A trap of booby birds struck the water with knifelike precision on their vertical kamikaze dives.

Swims are changing with the season, too. I'm no longer sweating and dehydrated when I step from the sea. The water feels refreshing but not cold.

In the morning I swam for more than an hour—mostly freestyle and breaststroke, but at times, I paused to float on my back and gaze up at the sky. The Sea of Cortez was flat and calm. I stroked toward the estuary, joined by kayakers and stand-up paddle boarders taking advantage of the smooth water. The water was so clear, like I was swimming through an aquarium. Huge schools of different fish swam around—black and white-striped sergeant majors, blue fish with yellow fins and baby trumpetfish—especially where the bottom was rocky and rife with plants. As I stroked through the water, I saw a wide-eyed puffer fish flutter its yellow fins below me. Obelisk-shaped blue fish with bright yellow fins nibbled on my toes and inner thighs. I'd turn around and make faces and underwater sounds and they would scatter, and as soon as I'd start swimming, they'd nibble on me again. It became a fun game.

Toward the end of my swim, I saw what I thought was a dolphin but soon realized it was a sea lion. First its head surfaced and then its blubbery body. Then with a swish of its tail, it submerged again. I watched it from the water and then later from my chair on the beach.

On Friday the 13th, I planned to kayak at 6 AM to watch the sun rise. But I overslept and awoke to see a huge spider on the wall. After throwing a shoe at it and missing three times, I grabbed the broom and finished the job. I think it was a wolf spider and not a venomous brown recluse, but whatever it was, one of us had to go.

Fortunately, the spider episode notwithstanding, stressful experiences in México had been few and far between. Most recently, Tropical Storm Lydia had blown through. I had been alone with no power for more than 24 hours.

Then days after we bought the condo in August, workers I'd hired to install a locked closet in the Master bedroom punctured a gas line. I'd been working on my computer when suddenly, the three male workers, talking loudly in Spanish, ran from the condo. I had no idea what they were saying but when the scent of gas assaulted me, I hightailed it out the door right behind them.

The situation quickly escalated into a nightmare. My husband was in Tucson. No one spoke English. I had become semi-fluent in Spanish back in the 90s when I lived in Peru, but that had been decades ago. I ran around the property until I found a maintenance worker and got him to turn off the gas to our unit.

I stood outside the condo, listening to everyone talking at once. The general manager, José, wanted to know if I had condo insurance. I think so, I said. I'd never even met him before and now I'd met him under the worst of circumstances. The gray-haired, head of maintenance (also named José) asked me in a surly voice why I hadn't consulted with him before starting this project. It honestly hadn't occurred to me. The contractor had assured me he worked often on condos around the property.

Tears streamed down my face as José continued to grill me. The sudden onslaught of culture shock and loneliness overwhelmed me. How I wished Chris was with me. He could have provided some comfort, but little help with the language barrier confusion. His repertoire of Spanish consisted of *Buenos Días* and *Cerveza, por favor*.

Jorge, a bearded, 30-something maintenance worker, spoke to me, his dark eyes wide with worry. And compassion. He said everything would be all right. They would fix this. The tears stopped flowing and I regained my composure.

And things did work out, eventually. The Bahía Delfín workers repaired the gas line and patched the wall. A day later, the closet was installed. The carpenter asked for extra money. Why? I felt like he should have accepted responsibility for the problem his workers caused. But apparently that's not how it works in México. I finally agreed to pay half of what he asked for.

Maybe that's the trick to adapting to life anywhere. Learning to accept what is wrong with a place without fighting it too much. I'd been fighting against the currents of life in the States for many years. México appealed to me in many ways, but I'd have to decide how I'd handle myself in stressful situations. When things went wrong, would I allow them to thrust me into the same state of frustration and disillusionment I had so often felt in the U.S.?

I grabbed my paddle and a bottle of water and walked down to the beach to unlock my kayak. I dragged it down the beach and kayaked out to Pastel Island—just over a mile offshore from the beach. The islands near San Carlos all have unique shapes—Peruana like a slope, Pastel flat and almost like a cake, Window Rock a jutting peak with a window offering a view of open sea. Honeymoon Island is the largest nearby island with ground fertile enough for cactus to grow. The islands are also nesting sites for sea birds and protected by the Mexican government. But what fascinates me the most about the islands is their absence of people. They're small expanses of space free of power lines, roads, buildings, and other evidence of human activity.

It took about 45 minutes to reach Pastel Island in my clunky boat—an Amazon special—bright red, heavy and wide— almost like a bathtub, really—with little ability to track in currents.

The resident pelicans on the island protested and took flight when I glided toward shore and beached my unwieldy craft. I exchanged hat and sunglasses for my swim cap and goggles. Floating over rocks and seaweed, I saw stingrays waving through the water, pairs of orange and black French angelfish, and blue triggerfish flapping their top and bottom fins to move through the water. I nosed through schools of silvery white minnows so numerous—there must have been millions of them—I couldn't see what was beyond them in the water. On the other side of the island, I swam through schools of tuna, yellow snapper, and luminescent green fish with black stripes.

Back in my kayak, I paddled out to Window Rock and met up with a boat full of people from Tucson. They allowed me to tie on to their boat since there was no place to land my kayak. We all hit the water, me wearing a cap and goggles, the adults and children on the boat in full snorkeling gear. The visibility here was so-so, but some of the rocks around the jagged rocky islands were covered with brown-orange cushion starfish.

After about 30 minutes in the water, I heaved myself back up on my kayak, said goodbye to my new friends, and paddled back to Bahía Delfín. By the time I hit the beach, I'd been on the water for four hours and my stomach rumbled loudly for lunch. But the earlier stress of the day was long forgotten. My time on the water had brought my being back into balance and reminded me why I was here. I could handle anything if I had the sea to turn to for solace.

CHAPTER FOURTEEN

Big Corn Island, Nicaragua – May-June 2016

"One learns first of all in beach living the art of shedding; how
little one can get along with, not how much. Physical
shedding to begin with, which then mysteriously spreads into
other fields."
Gift from the Sea – Anne Morrow Lindbergh

Every morning, I awoke at 5 AM, donned my swimsuit, and
walked down the coconut palm and conch shell-lined path to
the quiet beach. Usually there wasn't a breath of wind or a
ripple on the endless expanse of Caribbean Sea.

I'd wade into the shallows and swim for an hour. Just
knowing I'd get to swim every morning felt like a miracle. The
most open water swimming I'd ever done had been the
previous year when we'd flown to Greece for a group event
with the Big Blue Swim in the Ionian islands. I'd never seen
water so blue and crystal clear since then, until now in

Nicaragua. In Greece, I'd seen amazing limestone structures and caves and enjoyed the camaraderie of swimming every day with other water enthusiasts. But disappointingly, I'd seen more trash on the bottom than fish. Here, the water teemed with life.

The remnants of three sunken boats were visible from the beach in front of our hotel. Two jutted from the water just offshore. It took about twenty minutes to swim south to the wreck I had nicknamed "Shark Fin" rock, which marked the third resting place. On such a peaceful morning, it was difficult to imagine the sea conditions these ill-fated captains must have faced.

The sea bottom around this third wreck is a mass of spectacular reef. It became my favorite swimming destination. I looked forward to seeing the variety of coral — brilliant red fire coral, gold elk-horn-like branches, and knobby white masses that looked like cauliflower. Brittle starfish with spiky orange tips often clung to reef ledges. I'd glide among schools of blue damselfish, parrotfish, and pairs of king angelfish, and search for a pouting nurse shark that often hid under a ledge. I found myself talking to the fish.

One morning on my way to the reef, I swam past a large school of spotted rays. I paused and watched spellbound as they flapped their water wings through the saline water, in graceful flight.

At the resort, I initially resented my spartan accommodations. If only I could be in my own bed or at least the Sheraton, I thought to myself as I squirmed under stiff sheets on the uncomfortable mattress. But by day four, I became captivated by the tranquility of the quiet and remote island with its sea and sand and tangle of tropical trees. The loudest noise I heard was kids shouting with glee while playing soccer or the hum of the generator when the power went off. The landscapers used machetes to trim the grass instead of a lawn mower, so yardwork yielded sweat but no sound.

By day five, the inconvenience of the power routinely being off for two hours every morning no longer bothered me. Instead of feeling disgruntled with my dingy room, I felt grateful to have found this beautiful place. I lived outdoors most of the time, surrounded by natural beauty. What more did I need than four walls, a bed, a shower, and a toilet?

The island is primarily populated by Black people. I'd heard the rumor that long ago, an African slave ship sunk off the coast and its prisoners swam ashore and took up residence. If it was true, swimming ability wasn't passed down to the later generations. People who rushed into the water to escape the oppressive heat — usually in clothes rather than swimsuits — never swam. They waded into the seawater and stood around.

A banner with the lotus flowers representing the seven chakras, which according to yoga philosophy are whirling disks of spiritual energy in different parts of the body — hung in front of the elevated yoga *shala*. The open space between the wooden floor and the thatched roof offered a stunning view of the enormous tropical trees surrounding us.

Some of the trees were close enough to touch, like the banana tree full to bursting with bunches of still-green bananas. Another tree hung heavy with fruit that look like pickles that Lucas said tasted sour. This Mimbro tree had long, fern-like leaves that splayed out from branches like lush-green stars. Large broad, waxy leaves marked a nearby Noni tree. A liter of liquid from the tree's fruit supposedly cost a hundred dollars. I never did get a taste. The gigantic mango tree was our favorite. Mangos crashed into the dense vegetation around us during our practice. After a session, we'd rush to gather the most recent offerings.

In this remote place, we had nature and peace and quiet plus the time to deeply connect with ourselves and others. It was so different from the bustle of American life. In 2010, Chris and I had bought a beautiful high-end stucco construction, red-tile-roofed house high on a hill in Oro Valley. Our new home had four bedrooms, a huge yard with a grassy lawn and mature trees. What I loved most was the enormous swimming pool. In recent years, I'd come to believe material possessions were the key to happiness but I soon learned that wasn't the case.

Once we were living in the house, I thought it would be amazing if we bought a luxury car or a sports car. I got both of my wishes. We bought a yellow Camaro and a silver Audi. It was exciting to acquire something new — at least for a few months until I became obsessed with acquiring another new possession. The fancy house and the flashy cars didn't bring me lasting happiness.

Those three life-changing weeks spent on Big Corn Island taught me that acquiring material things brought only ephemeral happiness, nothing that would last. Immersing myself in nature, morning sea swims, practicing yoga, and connecting to myself on a deep level gave me a more permanent contentment.

CHAPTER FIFTEEN

San Carlos, México – November 2017

It was still dark when I pushed off the beach in my kayak. Gliding over midnight blue water, I gazed up at the full moon peeking out from a cloud, then turned my back on it to paddle toward the El Soldado Estuary. The sky behind the volcanic mountains near the estuary brightened to a pale and then a glowing pink—then transformed into brilliant hues of orange and pink and red—while the moon dipped toward the horizon behind me.

The rugged volcanic mountains surrounding me are a constant reminder of the Sea of Cortez's volatile geologic history. The Pacific and North American tectonic plates divide the sea. About five million years ago, movement along these plate boundaries began to separate the Baja Peninsula from the North American continent. Along the East Pacific Rise, where new seafloor is constantly created, the sea continues to broaden. The widest part of the sea is 130 miles across.

Earthquakes are constantly propagated along these plate boundaries. Fortunately, we've never experienced anything other than minor tremors.

I glided with the current into the mouth of the estuary, trying not to disturb the dozens of pelicans, terns and herons resting on a nearby sandbar. I passed a small island, where a great blue heron paced nervously on his stilt-like legs, craning his long neck to look at me, debating whether to stay or fly. Another heron perched in the mangroves decided it didn't want to risk being so close to a human in a big red boat and took flight, scolding me as its broad wings carried it over the water.

Large fish swam in the shallow water below me. A small fish leaped from the water again and again. In pursuit was a larger fish, hungry for breakfast. Soon the splashing stopped. The circle of life — and death — in the wild went on.

The human world is harder to navigate. People can be critical. They want sameness in others, conformity. And I've always been unique. Nature has a different opinion. So many times, I've watched a sunset or swum in the sea or clawed my way to the summit of a mountain. In all of those instances, I experienced cozy *I'm okay* comfort.

But why did this acceptance of myself so often fade away when I returned to real life? Maybe I needed to ask God these questions. I wasn't the same person I once was. I had found some new truths. I was walking a less materialistic path. I acted more selflessly than I once had. And I no longer wanted to run away, to take another exotic trip to find myself. I had found a place I called home. I felt a sense of peace and balance and awareness from this connection I felt with nature. *I belong here.*

I hear divine messages in every bird call, rolling wave, and round of dolphin chatter. *You're a part of this natural world.* This isn't an exclusive club. Everyone is invited to join. The only requirements are that you cherish the natural world, respect and care for other living beings that share the planet with you, and do your best to take care of them.

CHAPTER SIXTEEN

Big Corn Island, Nicaragua – May-June 2016

The heat was oppressive during the yoga sessions. The *shala* was far from the beach and we didn't feel even a breath of wind while the temperature climbed higher and higher as the day went on.

Every day opened with a two-hour Ashtanga modified primary series practice. Then we had an hour for breakfast. After lectures and workshops on anatomy and physiology and yoga philosophy—broken up by lunch and a one hour "peace hour"—which I typically spent in the sea to cool off—our days ended with a 90-minute Rocket class, which was essentially Power Yoga. I found this class way too intense for the end of the day.

I've always been a morning exerciser. I always do all my high-intensity training early in the day. Nearly four hours a day of yoga was overtaxing my body, especially in the intense heat.

A sore spot along my lower spine made me flinch whenever I put any pressure on it.

During the Rocket class, my body felt on the brink of collapse. I watched everyone do headstands and wanted to scream. I couldn't do one to save my life. The competitive side of me couldn't stand this. I'm strong and fit, I told myself. *So why can't I do a damn headstand?* I felt compelled to try to force it to happen even though I knew that was a terrible idea.

Once the class ended, I trudged back to my room, physically and emotionally depleted. After a shower and dinner, I returned to my room instead of lingering to socialize.

I studied the two training manuals we'd been given. I came across a discussion that warned that poses shouldn't be forced and that encouraged yogis to wait until the right time to do them. "Be gentle with yourself," the book encouraged, which was far from the attitude I'd been adopting. There was another phrase that stayed with me, that I often now share with my classes. "The true challenge is not can you do a headstand, but can you apply yoga to your life?"

Yoga is about connecting the body and breath, about understanding yourself better. It really didn't matter whether I could do a headstand or not. I wasn't there to compete with my colleagues or to prove anything to anyone. I'd come to learn to teach yoga well, to learn about myself, to establish a regular practice and then grow it in a way that worked for me and my students.

I had tried to apply yoga to my life in recent months. Occasionally, I experienced a more balanced state of being. More often, though, I engaged in old patterns of living that needed breaking, like talking and thinking negatively, and judging myself and others too harshly. The fact that I'd allowed my Masters swimming life to evolve into a mire of misery was proof that I was on the wrong path, that I needed to rethink my direction.

I have since learned that trying to keep up with or compare myself to others is self-destructive. My eyes don't need to be on a person doing that perfect headstand, a competitor in a nearby pool lane, or a turtle rescue volunteer that can do twice as much work as me. Weighing myself against others leads to feelings of inadequacy. Establishing my own goals and living in a way that keeps me on the path I've defined for myself leads to harmony and contentment.

Samskaras or ingrained patterns of thinking had been mentioned in a yoga philosophy session. I thought for a long while about which thinking patterns I needed to change and came up with quite a long list. First and foremost—I needed to learn to focus on positive things rather than the negative. I needed to learn to be satisfied with the simple, good things in life instead of depending on material possessions and money for happiness. I wanted to follow a spiritual path to contentment. And finally, I wanted to bring joy back into my swimming.

Masters swimming had served a purpose—it had helped me get through my father's illness and cope with losing him. But it wasn't serving me anymore. Away from the pool and competition, I'd begun to reconnect with the water by immersing myself in the sea just steps from my front door.

Rejuvenating. That's the best word for me to describe swimming in open water. Each morning, I'd wade in feeling sluggish, my body achy and stiff and I'd wade out feeling light and free and youthful again. Every day, I felt so blissfully happy I wanted to leap into the air and shout, "Yes! This is living."

I could swim hundreds of yards offshore and the water was still barely over my head. The sea on this leeward side of the island was smooth as glass, and there wasn't a single boat out on the water. I stroked four or five hundred yards offshore and flipped over on my back and soaked up the view of the island. The sandy earth was overgrown with sea grapes and palmetto palms. Bowing coconut palms tangled amongst lushly leafed fruit trees. I saw the beached blue and white fishing boat, and the bright blue Buccaneer sign off in the distance. Above the canopy of trees, the sun peeked out above a billowing mass of clouds.

The sea had revitalized my love for swimming. There were no intervals to obsess about, no teammates to race, and there was no need to finish my workout in a rush so the next group could start. I simply swam and explored, savoring the pure joy of moving through the water. Maybe there was merit in this kind of swimming, which was more like water play than training. Maybe it made more sense for my life right now. I was 53 and experiencing menopause. Maybe my body needed to be nurtured instead of beaten up.

Swimming in the sea had awakened me to a new way of experiencing the water. This way brought my being into harmony with the natural world around me. And it left me feeling at peace. The days of forcing my body to obey were over.

CHAPTER SEVENTEEN

San Carlos, México – 2017-present

Dolphins don't pop pills or rush to the hospital when they're sick. They don't need expensive imaging machines to diagnose internal abnormalities. Instead, they use their echolocation skills to scan the bodies of dolphins and humans around them, discerning whether an individual is pregnant, injured, or ill. Dolphins bounce back quickly from major injuries. They have an innate ability to heal themselves. Physician Michael Zasloff described the dolphins' ability to heal as regeneration rather than repair in Susan Casey's *Voices in the Ocean*. Football-sized injuries have healed without leaving any permanent deformity.

Dolphins can control their blood sugar levels at will. Research at the National Marine Mammal Association in San Diego indicated that dolphins flip a biochemical switch from Type 2 diabetic-like to normal states to compensate for insulin imbalances during long fasts or after ingestion of large amounts of fish.

Mankind is the biggest threat to dolphin health — and the well-being of thousands of other marine species. Our seas and oceans are quickly transforming from pristine waters into dumping grounds. Oil spills, sewage leaks, and agricultural runoff all contaminate the water, killing sea creatures and inducing unhealthy algal blooms. Careless boat captains and beach visitors toss litter on the sand or in the water, resulting in mountains of plastic waste piling up on beaches and swirling around in oceans.

I noticed there was a trash problem on the beach soon after we moved into our condo. Since then, I always pick up cans, bottles, cups, plastic bags, and other junk on San Francisco Beach in San Carlos and remove trash I see on the bottom or surface of the water whenever swimming or kayaking. It's a very small contribution — but something all of us can do easily. Small acts of care for the earth on the parts of many individuals can make a major impact.

Journalist Emily Bregel wrote articles for the Arizona newspapers about the water and sewage crisis in the Guaymas and San Carlos areas. The *Comisión Estatal de Agua* or CEA, our local water company, is inefficient and tends to put out fires instead of replacing failing infrastructure according to a presenter at the San Carlos country club, who also said that as much as 40 percent of local water is wasted due to leakage. With most of the nation's water allocated for mining and agriculture, residential water is often turned off for up to a week at a time during summer months.

Most residents who can afford them have water storage tanks known as *tinacos* installed in their homes that provide a back-up water supply in case of such an outage. At Bahía Delfín, we are fortunate because we have a large underground storage tank. Whenever this runs dry, our management trucks in water. Due to failing infrastructure and the outdated treatment plants, sewage leaks are common in many neighborhoods. Odor and illness often result. And there are many places where sewage is flowing straight into the sea.

Retired archaeologist Laurie Slawson owned a home in San Carlos for 11 years and now lives full-time in Tucson. She said the sewage problem was one reason she decided to sell her home. She was also distressed by the crime, noise, water outages, and constant trash left in the streets and on beaches. "There was a break in the sewer line at the street between my house and the neighbors'." She described the awful smell. "CEA never responded to multiple complaints."

Real estate companies and developers continue to market homes and condominiums in the area as if it's a paradise immune to problems. And many naïve buyers purchase without realizing what they're getting into or that they'll be placing an additional burden on an already-overtaxed water and sewer system.

The magnitude of our human carelessness jeopardizes the health of dolphins, sea lions, sea turtles, and many other sea creatures. Dead dolphins wash up in California with horrible skin lesions. In Europe, many perish from herpes and other autoimmune diseases. Cancers kill dolphins in Florida even though cetaceans are gifted with tumor suppressor genes. Apparently, there is only so much their bodies can do when they are bombarded by so many toxins. Dolphins in waters worldwide absorb pesticides, heavy metals, flame retardants, and other pollutants. When dead dolphins wash up on beaches, their chemical-laden bodies must often be disposed of as hazardous waste.

Dolphins often suffer from fatal intestinal blockages after ingesting foreign objects they mistake for food. Bottle caps, coffee cups, cigarette lighters, balloons and other toys, steel wool, nails, and chunks of asphalt have all been found in the bodies of dead dolphins.

Dolphins also suffer from emotional trauma due to acoustical bombardment from drilling, offshore construction, oil surveying, explosions, military exercises, and boat and ship engines. Sound travels further and 4.3 times faster in water than in air. Excessive noise damages dolphin mental health, hearing, and the nervous system. It also disrupts dolphin communications — required for hunting and mating and every other aspect of their lives.

If you think about noises that drive you nuts magnified exponentially and bombarding your brain constantly, with no breaks for sleep or mental recovery, you might be able to empathize with how traumatic the underwater environment has become for dolphins.

A 2017 article in the *Journal of Experimental Biology* showed that bottlenose dolphins and other whales overexert themselves to escape underwater noises. Decompression-free diving is normal for cetaceans. Panic to escape noise pollution causes them to dive down too fast or for too long and this prevents them from clearing their bodies of nitrogen effectively. Cuvier's beaked whales that dove more than 1000 meters below the surface of the water and remained at depth for more than an hour experienced decompression sickness. Beached mammals have shown evidence of gas and bleeding eyes and ears from nitrogen-gas-related embolisms.

Air guns used by petroleum companies to prospect the seafloor discharge 250-decibel blasts every ten seconds for months at a time. To offer some perspective on this — human eardrums burst at 185 decibels and the bombing of Hiroshima was measured at 248 decibels.

Navy sonar causes large numbers of cetaceans to dive too deep in panic and then beach themselves in large numbers.

Despite these disturbing statistics, the U.S. Military continues to fight against even modest restrictions on their activities.

Is there any hope that humans will eventually take compassion on these dolphins that are perpetually victimized by our sense of superiority and thoughtlessness?

CHAPTER EIGHTEEN

San Carlos, México – 2017–present

I've heard whistles, squeaks, clicks and a variety of other dolphin chatter. I've watched the dolphins catch fish (sometimes teaming up with pelicans), get high chewing pufferfish, body surf, chase each other, propel themselves high into the air, slap the water with their tails, bring garbage to me to remove, wear seaweed for a necklace, and rub fins. Many scratches on their bodies are the result of their intimate social behavior. Pectoral fin rubbing, pectoral-to-pectoral "handholding," and body rubbing are common in touchy-feely dolphin communities. Scientists, including Diana Reiss, have proven that dolphins recognize themselves in a mirror. They laugh, use tools, perform rescues, and enjoy music.

They also demonstrate affection and love for their dolphin companions and show signs of mourning when a loved one is lost. Dolphins reportedly have three times more von Economo neurons (VENs) than humans. These are specialized spindle-shaped cells in the brain responsible for empathy, intuition, communication, and self-awareness.

Lori Marino and other researchers believe dolphins experience an intimate connection with their pod members far deeper than even our strongest human relationships. They may live in distinct bodies, but it is as if they think and operate with one mind. Dolphins and whales strand themselves in large groups when one or two individuals are ill. If they are herded into an area to be slaughtered, they huddle together instead of trying to escape.

Paleoneurologist Harry Jerison referred to this shared oneness dolphins experience as "the communal self." He believed dolphins relate to others in a shared existence that we humans can't comprehend.

In addition to risking their lives for members of their own species, dolphins save humans on a regular basis as well. There are hundreds of reports of dolphins rescuing humans and even dogs from peril in the water. Below are a few of my favorites — some can be viewed on this YouTube video, 8 Most Unbelievable Dolphin Rescue Stories: https://www.youtube.com/watch?v=vrFw31UKb68.

In 2014, Adam Walker was swimming in the Cook Straight of New Zealand when a great white shark circled around him. Several dolphins appeared and remained close until the shark swam away and then stayed with him for another hour.

In 2007, a pod of bottlenose dolphins obstructed sharks from further injuring surfer Todd Endris. They escorted him to shore so he could seek first aid.

In 2012, a research vessel near Los Angeles, including marine biologist Maddelena Bearzi, followed a pod of bottlenose dolphins. Suddenly, one dolphin split off from the group and headed to deeper waters. Soon the rest of the dolphins followed. About three miles offshore, the dolphins formed a ring around the limp body of a teenage girl. The girl — later identified as a German tourist — was pulled from the water. A plastic bag around her neck held a suicide note. She was transported to a medical facility.

On December 26, 2004, a 9.1 magnitude earthquake caused tsunamis throughout coastal Asia. Two hundred eighty thousand people perished. Filipino diver Chris Cruz was leading dive teams from a boat offshore from Thailand when he received radio reports of an earthquake in Indonesia. Many dolphins surrounded their boat and started jumping. They appeared to be beckoning the boat to head offshore. Cruz ordered the boat captain to follow them. The dolphins led them away from the islands and out into deep waters where the boat remained safe from the tidal waves, which are only dangerous close to shore.

Dolphins haven't read the book of Matthew in the Bible, but they know the principle of the Golden Rule. They protect each other and when they see humans and even dogs in need of support, they treat us as they would want to be treated. Unfortunately, humans often don't extend that same courtesy to dolphins.

Dolphins have been shot, stabbed with knives and screwdrivers, pierced by spearguns, attacked with explosives, and purposely run over by Jet Skis. Many fishermen drag the waters with gillnets, which glean not only desired treasures from the sea but also bycatch — creatures unintentionally caught.

World-renowned cetacean expert Dr. Putu Mustika engaged in a study led by Dr. Charles Anderson of the Maldives Marine Research Institute. The results show that 4.1 million dolphins have been unintentionally caught between 1950 and 2018. The World Wildlife Fund (WWF) has stated that entanglement in fishing gear is the leading threat to whales and dolphins worldwide.

The Centro de Rescate Rehabilitación e Investigación de Fauna Silvestre AC (CRRIFS), a marine life rescue group I volunteer with, often receives reports of entangled marine animals, including dolphins, sea turtles, and sea lions. In the summer of 2019, a green turtle was brought to our facility. One flipper had been entangled in a net and was damaged to the point it had to be amputated. After the sea turtle recovered from surgery, a group of us went on a boat out to Peruana Island to release it. The turtle quickly compensated for the lost limb and disappeared into the depths to a cheering audience.

Although dolphins find chasing and outrunning boats distracting entertainment, they often are maimed or killed when struck by propellers. I gasp in horror from the beach as boats and Jet Skis swerve toward groups of dolphins or rapidly shift into reverse. I don't imagine these boat owners who chase the dolphins day after day ever consider investing in prop covers.

History shows that people in power have more desire to exploit the earth and the dolphins than care for them. Scientists use them as research subjects to glean data and publish articles. Companies like Sea World exploit them to fatten their wallets. The U.S. Navy and military groups from other countries train dolphins to locate underwater explosives and submarines and engage in other perilous work.

Dolphins aren't treated as intelligent beings or equals or as if their lives have value—they're treated like dispensable slaves. Man tends to adopt an egotistical point of view that humans are the smartest and have all the power and other living things are here on earth to do our bidding. Why this is considered acceptable, I'll never understand.

Dr. John Lilly conducted science experiments on dolphins beginning in the 1960s, killing and causing terrible suffering for countless dolphins. He even gave some of them LSD. One woman he hired, Margaret Howe Lovatt, manually stimulated an often-amorous dolphin she had been working with, given the name Peter. A scandal erupted and the ensuing separation from his love interest caused so much confusion and frustration for the dolphin that he committed suicide.

P.T. Barnum paid to have beluga whales delivered to entertain circus crowds and wasn't concerned that these creatures rarely survived for more than a day under his care. Hundreds died, yet the show went on.

Marine parks have become a multibillion dollar industry worldwide. Dolphins often suffer from severe depression in captivity. Depressed humans sometimes do crazy things under extreme emotional duress and dolphins behave similarly. There are countless recorded cases of dolphins and orcas biting and even killing trainers and water park visitors. Since such instances rarely happen in the wild, scientists have deduced that these aggressive acts are related to stress-related frustration and emotional imbalance. These dolphins experience great loss after being snatched away from their families. They experience emotional suffering we might be able to empathize with if we imagined ourselves being dragged away from beloved family members and our comfortable, familiar homes and tossed into a cage.

Every year in Taiji, Japan, over a span of about six months, thousands of dolphins are herded into a cove and slaughtered in a very cruel and inhumane way. Some are sold to commercial establishments. This hateful and thoughtless execution of dolphins — their only crime that they, like us, consume fish — has been going on since 1969. Marine mammal enthusiasts and activists worldwide have been outraged by this event.

American activist Ric O'Barry appeared in a documentary about the hunt entitled *The Cove*. Yet even efforts such as this haven't been able to stop the atrocities inflicted on these intelligent creatures.

Once land creatures, dolphins retreated to the water and started a new way of living 55 million years ago. Two hundred thousand years ago, man arrived and has wreaked havoc on the planet ever since. Is there any hope that people will change their habits for the sake of the dolphins they worship and admire? One of my daily prayers is that one day it will happen.

CHAPTER NINETEEN

Big Corn Island, Nicaragua - May 26, 2016

I awoke to aching muscles and a sore spine, desperate for a sea dip. After slipping on my swimsuit, I stumbled down to the beach. Waves crashed on the shore and ominous dark clouds gathered overhead. The color of the sea constantly shifts with the time of day and weather. When the water is flat and calm before the sun rises, it is the color of sand. Overcast or stormy skies paint it shades of gray. On sunny afternoons when I swam during our peace hour, the water sparkled in hues of turquoise and aquamarine.

Once I immersed myself in the sea, the tension in my body ebbed away. After swimming to and from the reef, I flipped over on my back, floating, my body's boundaries mingling with the surrounding sea. Always when I am alone with nature, I feel at peace, acceptable, as if there is nothing about who I am that needs changing.

Now that I'm further on my spiritual journey, I believe that we are all close to flawless in our true form. Now I know that I often dislike myself when I'm around others because I'm out-of-kilter somehow. I really am a better person when I'm in a state of harmony. Nature brings me the calm and balance I need to experience my authentic self and feel a connection to a Divine presence. Maybe for someone else writing or playing a musical instrument would make that happen. Every person can connect with their true being if they achieve a state of balance and calm. Praying can make this happen, especially when it involves mostly listening. The chatter in the mind must cease to experience it. With practice, it is possible to achieve this state of harmony under a variety of circumstances.

I know from experience how easy it is to descend into a state of utter blackness. When it happens, all hope seems lost. I don't feel kind and loving. I want to lash out at the world around me. Self-loathing threatens to strangle me. Thoughts that maybe life isn't worth living creep in. I've been there often enough—before I drew closer to God and even since then—but I am now confident that the light will return. That helps me to step outside to a quiet place where I can commune with nature and continue praying, continue meditating, continue immersing myself in water until my authentic self and the natural light in my consciousness returns. I say this in loving hope that anyone facing a similar darkness will forge on, will not give up, will ask God or a friend or family member for help, will recognize that there will be a new, promising day on the horizon.

The sky darkened and light rain pelted my skin as I walked up the beach to my room. Minutes later, rain thundered on my roof. The sound of torrential rain soothed me, and I felt safe and cozy inside my room. I let out a sigh of contentment, and marveled that something so simple as a rainy morning could bring me joy. I had all my belongings organized in the old armoire, nothing out of place or extraneous. I looked forward to quiet moments after my swims where I sat on the edge of my bed, sipped Chai tea and studied my training manual or listened to music on my iPad.

Skirting puddles and coconut palms that might drop heavy fruit on my head, I walked to the yoga *shala*. I'd been placing my mat in the front lately because when I couldn't see anyone else, I found it easier to focus on my own practice. I'd memorized the Ashtanga modified primary series and that particular day, my practice flowed very naturally. Maybe it was hearing the soothing patter of rain on the leaves and thatched roof above us. Images of the ocean flowed through my mind. Moving through the poses almost felt like moving through the water, fluid and effortless.

During my swim, I had thought about Melissa and how skilled she was at yoga. She wore her hair short in a way that highlighted her beautiful facial features and was very petite and lean. She looked amazingly graceful and relaxed performing the postures. I imagined yoga must be to Melissa what swimming was to me. A refuge. It was clear she'd spent years acquiring her skills.

Pondering Melissa's road to mastery helped me to recognize I was on a journey too: to learn yoga and to be gentler to myself. I'd taught many children and adults how to swim and knew from experience it took years for a swimmer to master every stroke. Since I'd only practiced yoga regularly for three months, I recognized it would take time to master the postures. I felt grateful to be attending a training where I could focus completely on yoga. It would give me more time and space to become a skilled teacher and to establish my own practice.

By late morning, the heavy clouds dispersed, and the scorching equatorial sun reappeared. During peace hour, I dashed into the water. I stroked my way out to the wreck just offshore from our hotel. I thought I saw movement on the algae-covered hull and then realized with amazement that I was seeing an octopus. I later learned how highly intelligent these nine-brained creatures are from watching the Netflix documentary, *My Octopus Teacher*, and reading *The Soul of an Octopus*.

The mysterious creature blended in with the green, red, and brown algae that consumed what remained of the ship's hull. The bulging body flashed purple, while its red and brown tentacles seemed to flow as it moved ghost-like across the surface of the ship. It was like watching a graceful dance.

At my favorite reef, three plate-sized, blue iridescent triggerfish swam by, flapping their top and bottom fins. They looked like a stingray moving in a vertical position. I spotted two crabs mating on the bow of the "shark fin" wreck.

I got permission to observe instead of taking the afternoon Rocket class. Ashley sat beside me, also observing. We had been told that we could suggest small adjustments for the safety of the participants. I had walked over to help someone when Lucas ordered me to sit down in a very severe voice.

He rolled his eyes at me when I made eye contact with him. I couldn't understand why he had taken such a dislike to me. Did he find my 30 years of fitness teaching experience intimidating? I had a vague impression that the man lacked confidence. His constant irritation with me was frustrating. Ashley was still walking around helping people. He hadn't ordered her to sit down.

I'd hoped to be inspired by a yogi who could help me grow personally and spiritually. Chelsea—the assistant instructor—was kind, compassionate, and gentle. I had never met anyone quite like her. She seemed to exist in a state of steady and serene peace. She spoke in a calm, soothing voice. She had left a long-term relationship in Florida to live a much simpler life in Nicaragua. She exhibited many qualities I admired.

Lucas came to class dressed in raggedy cut-off jeans and ripped up T-shirts. The leader that I anticipated would become a role model was more like the wind—constantly changing direction. He'd want to hug me one minute, then snap at me the next.

Exhausted from the day's earlier sessions, I found it impossible to let go of the frustration and anger I felt over his harsh words. Tears welled up in my eyes as I waited for the class to end as the sky flashed brilliant orange and then faded into darkness.

I soon learned my instincts about Lucas were correct. After training ended one day, Lucas invited our group to go to dinner on the other side of the island. I figured the outing would include heavy drinking, which didn't interest me. I wanted to finish the day with a nourishing meal and then return to studying. I wasn't the only one to decline Lucas's invitation. Melissa and Danielle also stayed behind.

The next morning, I returned from my swim to find Ashley sitting in the restaurant drinking a beer. I could tell when I spoke to her that something was wrong. But she only shrugged when I asked. At breakfast, everyone looked either hung over or upset. Chelsea's face was stained with tears. The usually smooth space between Danielle's brows were creased in anger. She and Kyle usually sat beside each other, shoulders touching. Today, Danielle sat a distance away, avoiding eye contact with him. Melissa's eyes brimmed with tears. At first no one wanted to talk about it. They all seemed to be in a state of shock.

The cause of everyone's distress was Lucas. During dinner, he imbibed to the point of drunkenness, wanting to celebrate, he said, because the July class had 12 participants. It was all about money. He would be getting lots of money and so he wanted to get drunk.

Lucas had bought a bottle of tequila and asked everyone to take shots with him. He became belligerent when anyone refused. I probably would have punched him if he'd tried to pressure me—I held so much pent-up resentment about the way he'd been acting.

Eventually, the others gave in and downed some shots. And this is where it transported them. To a place of disillusionment and despair. My hands shook with rage. What was wrong with this man? He had a class to teach, students here and now that wanted to learn. Couldn't he make any effort to be a decent role model instead of decimating everyone's morale?

Melissa seemed to take it the hardest. It was obvious she had thought Lucas was much more than what he was. She wanted to go home, she said. I empathized with her and with the others. I once thought I'd found a writing mentor and had been gravely disappointed when he lost interest in helping me. But I'd moved past the disappointment and gone on to publish hundreds of articles and many books. A mentor would have been nice, but finding creative ways to learn, writing daily, and using different strategies to keep the flame of my motivation burning have sufficed.

Al Jarreau has been my biggest hero. His music first inspired me when I heard "After All" my junior year at Clemson. Until he passed way in 2017, he continued to release songs I found uplifting. So many memories of my life's experiences bring to mind an Al Jarrea song.

My skin tingles whenever I hear Mornin' which reaches a crescendo when he sings about touching the face of God.

Hearing those words seems to create an instant Divine connection.

The man radiated spiritual energy. Whenever I saw him in concert — even two months before he left this earth — when he leaned against a stool, clearly experiencing back pain — he gifted us with his songs and his signature smile, his zest for life, radiating optimism and love.

I now understood what Lucas's variable moods were about. The man was an alcoholic. He had to stay off-site, so we wouldn't witness his nighttime drinking habits. Maybe his alcoholism and hurricane moods explained why he was in Nicaragua and his wife was in Europe.

I hoped my new yoga friends would find the strength to keep on going. They did, but their disciplined behavior evaporated.

Kayla drank nightly after that. Sometimes she was so hung over, she missed sessions. Ashley and Melissa also hit the wine bottle harder after that night. I wondered if any of them had hoped the daily disciplines of their yoga practice would empower them to gain more control over their choices. Maybe they simply threw in the towel after Lucas showed his true colors. I'll never know for sure, but I found the possibility disheartening.

I will be different. I will be a loving and accepting yoga teacher. I will teach with compassion. I will help people to overcome obstacles, grow spiritually, and discover their true authentic selves.

CHAPTER TWENTY

Tucson, Arizona and San Carlos, México
December 2017-January 2018

I drove back to Tucson often to visit Chris since he hadn't yet retired. But always, within a few days of returning to the States, I fell into a depressed funk. Eventually, my mind would go numb to the chaos, stress, and noise, so that I could function on a superficial level. During the rare moments of silence outside in our backyard, I longed to hear waves crashing on the sand, a cry of a gull.

I felt guilty for being despondent. I wanted to spend time with Chris and visit my mom and children. As much as I loved them all, I couldn't seem to maintain a state of calm in Tucson. Our neighbor across the street continued to open his garage every morning at six AM to load up pick-up trucks that drove to work sites. After that, he'd start loud sawing projects in his garage that would persist until late afternoon.

My mom always seemed to be in a hurry, which made me realize how much I wanted to avoid living a rushed lifestyle. I had no desire to be constantly worried about issues of day-to-day life.

My daughter—then in nursing school—began to adopt a hardened view of life, which I found discouraging. Age-related sickness and decline and death were "natural," she told me.

Day by day, little by little, I moved away from that space. I had started to study Christian Science again. I studied the daily Bible lessons and many articles on JSH-online. I contacted different Christian Science practitioners, asking them to pray for me. I wanted to be healed of the migraines. Fortunately, my condition had improved, but it always seemed to worsen whenever I returned to Tucson. What I needed more than anything was a closer relationship with God. I also needed to learn—through prayer and meditation—how to become less reactive and steadier emotionally.

Ritual and self-denial are often cited as pathways to grow closer to God. Those methods didn't work for me. I'd felt my Father/Mother's presence while stroking through the water, watching a sunset, savoring the color and scent of a beautiful flower. I had started to not only read Scriptures, but to ponder them while outdoors and I started to pray for my family and friends every morning whenever I swam.

When we returned to San Carlos after Christmas, I ran down to the beach to look at the sea. Usually, it's windy and choppy in the afternoons. But on this overcast day, the water was a flat calm. Conditions were favorable to swim, really swim, at 3 PM. I waded into the water, which was chillier than in November, but not unbearable sans wetsuit, and started swimming. I wanted to shout, such intense joy raced through my veins. That cool water caressed my brain and body, assuring me everything was all right. Feeling and smelling and tasting the sea again brought back my vitality and zest for life.

Chris stayed until January 7. Each night, as I watched the sun descend behind Tetakawi's jagged peak and the clouds over the ocean transform into layers of glowing pink cotton, a sense of gratitude warmed my heart. There was a problem, though. Chris didn't want to watch the sunsets. He found sea swimming unsettling. The beach and México weren't becoming his happy place the way they were for me.

I had settled into my new life in México. Not only was I a permanent resident, I had received documentation giving me legal permission to work. I taught yoga classes in our community and at a yoga studio in town. I also had made many friends. While I thrived teaching yoga classes, sea swimming, writing, and spending time outdoors, Chris often slept fitfully, felt tired and anxious, and became easily bored. His nose would run for hours after a sea swim. I wondered how we would work this out. I was happy here. He was miserable here. I was miserable in Tucson. That's where he wanted to be.

The night before he took a midnight bus back to Tucson, we enjoyed one last dinner. Later, we lay in bed snuggled up together talking and dozing for a couple of hours. At 10 PM I walked him out to the guard gate to meet his taxi driver. I felt groggy and more disengaged than I would have liked to be. I gave Chris a cursory hug. He stepped back and carried his backpack to the car. It's so strange how you can feel so much love for a person sometimes you feel you might burst. That's how I felt about Chris as I walked back to the condo alone. Realizing he was suddenly absent. Our lives had just diverged.

He didn't have cell service in México, so I couldn't find out if he had a good taxi ride, if the bus station was crowded, if the bus left on time at midnight. All night I tossed and turned, wishing I'd been more alert when I'd spoken to the taxi driver.

My Spanish was rusty. The driver had seemed to understand where to take Chris, but I hadn't been able to communicate much more than that. I should have said please drive carefully, told him that my husband's safety mattered to me. I lay awake, playing over and over again in my mind what I should have said.

By 9 AM the next morning, when Chris should have been asleep in our house in Tucson, I still hadn't received a text. I paced around. Burst into tears. Then I called the Tufesa bus office in Tucson. The bus hadn't yet crossed the border, the woman said. They wouldn't know the arrival time until that happened.

Three hours later, an incoming text finally flashed on my phone screen. But by then I had become too anxious, too tired, overwhelmed. A day earlier, Chris and I had been living together in our small condo — intimately connected — me aware of every detail about Chris's day — that he ran five miles, drank chocolate milk after workouts for recovery, and ate grain and nut cereal for breakfast — and once we had been separated, for more than fourteen hours, his state of existence had become a blank.

Only during our phone call that afternoon would I learn that the bus made so many stops he was unable to sleep during the night. He had had to exit the bus and stand around in Nogales, Sonora, for hours before re-boarding again, this time with a different driver, to cross the border. But he had made it back to Tucson. Where he wanted to be. And I sat on the couch in our San Carlos condo, looking out at Tetakawi and a stretch of sea, missing Chris and at the same time knowing México was where I wanted to be.

CHAPTER TWENTY-ONE

Big Corn Island, Nicaragua – June 2016

One morning as I swam toward the reef, I was alarmed to see men spear fishing from a small boat. I'd never seen any boats near the reef before. No one on this sleepy island seemed to be awake before sunrise. I'd swum with these schools of fish for almost three weeks. They'd scattered the first time I encountered them. Now they often swam beside me, unafraid, as if I had become—despite my size and colorless skin—a member of their school. I felt guilty for earning their trust. Humans couldn't be trusted. Most took whatever they wanted from the sea. As the men in the small boat speared the water again and again, the water became turgid with sediment.

In the bright sunlight, I saw the men's silhouettes tossing what they'd caught into the back of the boat. Once the hunters left, I searched the reef for the nurse shark. I couldn't find him anywhere. Tears filled my goggles. What if they'd killed him? I knew people living on this island depended on fish for food, but this knowledge didn't diminish my sadness. I felt connected to these aquatic creatures. Their lives had begun to matter to me.

During my afternoon swim, rain pelted my arms and back. The rain and overcast weather calmed the fish. I found myself enveloped by them. I couldn't even see clear water—all I saw was thousands of silvery bodies flashing bright as they moved. It was as if the event with the spear fisher never happened. Maybe the fish distinguished me as safer to be around than the men who'd hunted them earlier.

I'd often seen a blue tang swimming among a large school of yellow-striped French grunts. These fish are brilliant blue, with yellow tails and black accents. Maybe the blue tang had lost her mother and didn't notice she appeared different from her fellow companions now that she'd been "adopted." If only all humans could be so accommodating—accepting and welcoming everyone regardless of skin color, nationality, sex, political views, or religion.

The underwater aquarium gave me an up-close view of a blue tang feeding on plants, a butterflyfish with a big black spot near its tail, a green pufferfish with hooded eyes, a pair of black and orange French Angelfish. Up close, their eyes look like yellow and black marbles. All the fish have pectoral fins that are delicate and fanlike. I didn't see them at first but then marveled at how they waved through the water like small wings.

A few times I'd swum against the current about two miles south to Arenas Beach. From the water, I'd spied white lounge chairs and blue umbrellas neatly arranged on a long stretch of beach. Primitive homes bracketed one end of this public beach, while a yellow colonial style mansion was positioned along the water at the other end. One enormous house sat nestled amidst a jungle of trees in the green hills, which looked lusher than ever after recent rains. The view of this beach was so inviting, I always wanted to linger, floating on the waves while admiring the view. Our yoga teacher training was coming to an end and our final exam would be tomorrow afternoon.

Three weeks of swimming in the Caribbean had given me my wish. I'd found joy in swimming again. Would I ever race again? Maybe. But training and competition wouldn't be my focus — it would be joy and savoring the experience of moving through water.

As I swam with the current back to the Paraiso, poetic thoughts drifted through my mind. *How many ways can I describe this love affair I have with the water? How can I express how each time I immerse myself in this soothing sea, I feel like I am reconnecting with my true being — the part that becomes lost after too much time trapped inside cement walls.*

I'd spent more hours in the sea over the course of these three weeks than I ever had in my life. I knew that after I returned to the United States, I'd long for this beloved sea, long to immerse my head in this salty water where I'd mingle with grunts, blue tang, angelfish, triggerfish, spotted eagle rays, and check in on my nurse shark friend. I'd begun to care about them and empathize with them. I hadn't cared that much about creatures in the natural world since my frog-loving days beside the Olentangy River.

I imagined that during my upcoming pool swims, I would find myself closing my eyes and trying to awaken in my imagination the salty smell of the sea, the gentle toss of the waves, and the sensation of being surrounded and supported by seawater. No swim in a chlorinated pool would ever deliver this kind of experience. The pool was water, which I loved. But the sea had become my new concept of paradise.

Soon, though, my days of sea swimming would end. An airplane would transport me far away from here. I would be a marine creature stolen from the sea.

CHAPTER TWENTY-TWO

San Carlos, México – January 18, 2018

"What if nature spoke to us in music, and the dolphins were her chorus? What if we stopped talking, and joined their harmony?"
Susan Casey – *Voices in the Ocean*

When I kayaked around the rocky point near the Delfinario (where dolphins and other marine creatures are held in captivity to entertain crowds), a low-lying layer of haze blocked my view of the Miramar beachfront homes lining the shore around the bay. But it was beautiful out on the sea, so calming to cruise along and see diamonds brought to life by sunlight on the water.

Thoughts of my family drifted through my mind as I paddled along. I sensed my solitude, my distance from them. Sadness hung heavy in my heart, like the haze over the water. It felt strange to be alone so much. It left hours for contemplation, which helped me understand myself better and helped me experience spiritual growth. But at the same time, I was missing opportunities for connection, to love and be loved.

Sometimes I got so absorbed in my new life by the sea, too many days would fly by before I'd realize I hadn't talked to my mom or children for a while. But during the morning kayak excursion, I saw my husband's face, my mom's face, and my children's faces in my mind's eye and thought about how deeply I loved them and how much I wanted them to be well and happy. I prayed for them and asked God and his angels to take care of them. I thought about others too — my stepdaughter Lisa and her family, my stepson Tom, my brother Dave, and my cousin Sam. It was a loving kindness meditation out on the sea.

I saw my son's thick, wavy hair — usually too long and hanging down into his eyes — his big dark eyes and his mile-long eyelashes. My daughter, her skin pale and smooth as a river pebble, her brown, lively, intelligent eyes gazing at me through round, gold-rimmed glasses. Chris, with his downy, almost white hair, warm hazel eyes peering at me through lenses that make him look smart and serious, his black T-shirt stretching across his broad, athletic chest. And my mom sitting out on her patio, wearing flowered Bermuda shorts, her legs still toned and shapely like a teenager's, her wispy gray hair blowing in the breeze as she watches birds eat from various feeders in her yard and remarks about a spot on her white shirt.

I saw each one of them as clearly as if they were with me gliding over the water. I felt connected to them despite being hundreds of miles away. It was a new experience feeling this sense of unity even from a distance.

As I've transitioned into a more spiritual state-of-mind, it has happened more and more frequently. Whenever I feel stressed out and my head is overrun with rambling thoughts, I can feel disconnected from a person sitting in the same room with me. It's about consciousness. When I'm calm and present and open, I can connect with someone in a manner I can't when I'm out of balance—even if our physical bodies are in different countries.

I wondered if I could ever connect on an intimate level with the dolphins. Would it require a miracle? Divine intervention? An underwater version of the Pentecost—described in the book of Acts where the Holy Spirit enabled the apostles to speak a mutually understood language—might bring dolphin and man into a meaningful conversation.

Dolphins can recognize their own faces in mirrors. They raise their heads from the water to see their reflections when experiencing a pufferfish high. They jump out of the water to get a higher vantage point, to see better what's happening above water or on the beach—such as what nearby humans are up to. I know for sure they check out dogs. Maybe they wonder if we're so kind to our furry friends, why we can't bestow this same love to other creatures on earth including them.

Always when I'm around dolphins, so many questions pop into my mind. Do they identify me differently than bathers who wade or occasionally swim? Do they notice the differences in our swimming proficiencies? Do they notice the lightness or darkness of our skin, the differing shapes of our bodies, our facial features? Or do we humans all look the same to them?

Dolphins have names. Their companions know them and call them by their names in dolphin speak. I wonder if they have assigned a name for me. She who never misses a day in the water? That land creature who can't stay away from the sea?

I wish I knew what name the dolphins have given me. Maybe it's a thread of whistles with a squeak at the end to punctuate it. I'll keep listening for sounds whenever a dolphin approaches. Maybe if I hear my dolphin name often enough, I'll be able to introduce myself with a streak of whistles and squeaks from now on.

CHAPTER TWENTY-THREE

Big Corn Island, Nicaragua – June 2016

My right knee went numb within minutes of starting afternoon Rocket class. I must have aggravated it trying the bind on the *Ardha Baddha Padma Paschimottanasana* for the first time in the morning session. This asana involves placing the bent knee on top of the opposite thigh at a very tight angle and then reaching around the back to grab the foot with the hand and creates some serious torque on the knee. Although most people have heard names of poses such as Downward-facing dog and Child's Pose, these asanas and others have equivalent names in Sanskrit.

Many moves in Rocket involved deep knee bends, which I didn't feel safe doing with my knee hurting. I asked Chelsea for permission to exit the class. After receiving her okay, I walked to the restaurant and asked for a bag of ice.

If it hadn't been raining buckets, I would have hobbled down to the sea for a therapeutic swim. Instead, I reclined on my room bed and listened to the rain thundering on the roof as if Noah's flood had returned. I worried if the knee worsened, I wouldn't be able to teach my practical exam session the next day.

Fortunately, I awoke the next morning free of pain and swam before Kayla and Kyle taught their exam classes. I took another long swim in the afternoon before it was my turn. I stroked all the way south to Arenas and stopped by the pier to look for the Go Pro Ashley had lost the previous day while on a stand-up paddleboard. I aborted my search and rescue plan after I found myself surrounded by enormous shiny silver barracuda. Razor sharp teeth hide behind those mean-looking lips. Barracuda don't frequently attack humans, but why they attack isn't well understood and when they do, there's plenty of blood involved. The water around me was murky and shadowed by the pillars of cement on the pier. I've seen my share of barracuda on dives and swims, but at that moment, terror lanced through me. For all I knew reef sharks also lurked in the murky depths. My instincts told me to split.

I stroked rapidly away from that creepy place to Arenas Beach. All the white lounge chairs were deserted. I stood in waist-deep water and caught my breath, badly in need of a stress break. I looked at my watch. There wasn't much time to dawdle. Barracudas and avoidance tactics hadn't figured into my plan. But there was no way I would swim past the end of that pier again.

I opted to swim under it in the shallower water. I swam past a group of young Nicaraguan boys that might have been eight or nine years old. Speaking in Spanish, I asked them their names and introduced myself. They laughed when I misheard one of their names. They asked about my mask and snorkel, and I lamely told them I breathed through the tube. That incited more boyish laughter. Their wet hair plastered to their heads, their eyes dark and wide, their smooth damp faces shone under the sun. Even though I felt foolish having them laugh at my expense, I valued this brief connection with the local people.

I glanced at my watch and winced. I would have to swim fast or I'd miss my teaching exam. I swam under one of the pier pylons close to shore. There was a fishing boat nearby. I waited until I knew they had me on their radar before swimming past. This pause delayed me even further. The instant I swam around the boat, I hauled at race pace back to the resort. I got back with only 30 minutes to shower and change. But I felt calm and in control from the exertion.

I downed a Powerade and most of a Coke before walking briskly to the *shala* to lead the class. I felt excited and invigorated by my long sea swim. I first expressed how much the weeks studying with the group had meant to me. I got a little teary and so did the others. Then I turned on a music playlist and started my class. The familiar music helped me relax and the class flowed naturally. I worried I might teach out of sequence or not finish all the asanas before the hour ended. But it all unfolded smoothly.

I will always remember how I shouted with glee when I finished the class, how everyone in the group hugged and congratulated me. Danielle said the class was less painful because of the music and that she enjoyed it. All the others said it had a nice flow and that the music was a good addition. It was one of those winning moments I wanted to never forget, where all the stars and planets seemed to align for success.

I walked back to my room and sang along to a couple of Al Jarreau songs to celebrate before showering and dressing for dinner. I would meet Chelsea and Lucas at the restaurant to hear their critiques of my class before the others arrived.

Fortunately, all the feedback was very good, which thrilled me. After all my hard work, I would pass the class and get my yoga teacher training certificate. I'd be able to start teaching at SaddleBrooke once I returned to Arizona.

The next day after Melissa and Danielle finished their practical exams, Lucas said we would take our written test right away.

Overall, everyone performed well on their practical teaching exams. Each class was unique and expressed the individual instructors' personalities. It had been inspiring to see each person's teaching styles develop during the weeks we were there. Kyle excelled at delivering clear, concise instructions, and both he and Ashley conducted classes with amazingly smooth transitions and a natural flow. Melissa's gentle, calm voice instantly relaxed me. Her soothing tone blended in with the sound of the wind in the trees and the birds and made me feel connected with nature during my practice. She executed every posture with so much skill and grace I could see how I could benefit from practicing yoga daily the way she had for years. She really inspired me.

After completing our written tests, we went to the *shala* to receive our teaching certificates. After all the build-up, Lucas said Chelsea had filled out the certificates incorrectly and they were invalid. I ground my teeth together in annoyance. Why didn't he fill out the certificates himself since he was the lead instructor? He would have, had he taken any pride in us at all.

He promised to mail the certificates within two weeks, which I didn't believe for a minute. I asked him if he could just sign the certificate in a different spot since I needed it to present to the gym where I'd be teaching. He rolled his eyes and said he had two empty certificates and that they could give me one of those.

I felt guilty for accepting the certificate when the others had worked equally hard for three weeks and had nothing to show for it. After Lucas passed out the fake certificates to everyone else, he wanted to take a bunch of photos. I found this annoying. He'd bitten my head off dozens of times over the course of the training when I'd tried to take photos and now suddenly, he wanted to take a million photos of us standing there holding (mostly) invalid certificates. I felt only coldness in his handshake and hug. It was all for show. I'd traveled all the way to Nicaragua to study yoga for emotional and spiritual growth and found my biggest challenge to be coping with a yogi leader who'd lost his way.

More than four months would pass before any of the other graduates received their certificates. I started teaching within a week of returning home, which I wouldn't have been allowed to do without a legitimate certificate and registration with the Yoga Alliance.

I left the island the next morning knowing I would never forget my little nurse shark (that I learned hadn't been killed by the fishermen after all) and all the other amazing sea creatures that I had encountered during my open water swims (although I could have done without the barracudas). I knew I would always remember Melissa's graceful movements, Ashley's perfectly executed headstands, Kyle's guitar-playing, Danielle's delicate beauty, and Kayla's laugh. But it would be Chelsea's freckled, slightly sunburned face, brilliant blue eyes, and joyous disposition that I would remember the most.

Heather Bixby and I display our High Point towels after the U.S. Masters Swimming Long Course Meters State Championship at the University of Arizona pool in 2016.

Race start (teal suit, second from left) at 2016 USMS Long Course Meters Summer Nationals in Portland, Oregon.

Performing Triangle pose (Utthita Trikonasana)at the 200-hour Yoga Teacher training on Big Corn Island, Nicaragua in 2016.

The Caribbean Sea, my sanctuary at the 2016 Yoga Teacher training on Big Corn Island.

Yoga practice at the YTT in the outdoor shala on Big Corn Island, 2016.

My daughter, Marion, holding a Red Cushion sea star underwater at Starfish Point in Grand Cayman (2017).

Bahia Delfin – the condo complex where we live in
San Carlos, Sonora, Mexico.

2017 San Carlos Sunset

Preparing for one of my daily morning swims in the
Sea of Cortez (2018).

One of many yoga photos taken by Laurie Slawson in
2018 on San Francisco beach for a U.S. Masters Swimming
article.

My son Keith and I near the El Soldado Estuary in 2018.

A celebratory hug with Anna after completing her December 2018 Yoga Nidra course in Puerto Vallarta.

Standing in front of a majestic Cardon cactus in San Jose, outside Guaymas, Sonora, Mexico (2018).

Marion and I near the Palapa Griego restaurant in San Carlos in 2018.

Hanging out with a friend, Mercedes Martinez, after the Cruz de Bahia Miramar 1600-meter swim race in 2018.

A 2018 tropical storm brought high winds and turbulent waters to San Carlos.

A swim with Nala and Maya at Vallarta Adventures in
Nuevo Vallarta, Mexico (2019).
Photo by Vallarta Adventures

Protection around sea turtle nest in San Carlos, Mexico (2019).

Baby Olive Ridley sea turtles about to be released by Centro de Rescate Rehabilitación e Investigación de Fauna Silvestre AC (CRRIFS) staff and volunteers in 2019.

Big turn out for a 2019 Centro de Rescate Rehabilitación e Investigación de Fauna Silvestre AC (CRRIFS) sea turtle release, conducted by Dr. Elsa Coria Galindo and other staff and volunteers.

Bottlenose Dolphins in San Carlos near El Soldado Estuary November 2019.

Chris and my mom outside a cabin in Pinos Altos, New Mexico (2019).

Friends Jose and Mercedes Martinez smile for a photo with a colorful rainbow in the background (2020).

Our newly adopted Chow Chow Chief arriving by plane in September, 2020.

Chief is now a happy member of our family.

My mom and I on the golf course near her house in
Oro Valley (2020).

Bottlenose Dolphins swimming together in the Sea of Cortez
waters around San Carlos (2019).

Chris and Marion and I took a beautiful hike to Seven Falls near Sabino Canyon in Tucson (2021).

I won the 55-59 age group in the 1600-meter swim at the Alcatraz/Cruz de Kino swim in 2022 after having set a course record in the same age group in 2019.

Dolphins all around me one summer morning in 2022.
Drone image by Fred Elling

Mirador in San Carlos. March, 2022.

CHAPTER TWENTY-FOUR

Nuevo Vallarta and San Carlos, México - 2019

I participated in a dolphin swim two years ago with Vallarta Adventures during a weeklong Nuevo Vallarta vacation. I say this, with an apology on my lips because I hate the idea of dolphins in captivity. But I wanted to touch and have an intimate experience with dolphins just once. I thought an up-close experience might teach me more about them.

Before signing up, I browsed the company website, which boasted that they only allowed the dolphins two hours per day of tourist interactions and they had certifications from Mexican environmental protection groups, including PROFEPA, and the facility was Humane Certified by American Humane in Washington, D.C., which requires the highest standards for animal captivity. Reading this didn't by any means exonerate me from guilt — I knew the dolphins were confined to a pool instead of the vast Pacific — but it made me feel a bit better.

Several other tourists signed up for the dolphin adventure. After a fun encounter with sea lions, where they splashed us a lot and imitated our facial expressions, we were taken to the big dolphin pool.

I swam most of the time with two female dolphins, Nala and Maya. We exchanged a kiss and a dance together. I rode on Mala's back, clutching one pectoral fin with one hand, the other holding onto her dorsal fin for the long distance swim underwater. My heart raced with anticipation. I forgot to inhale before Mala dove underwater and by the time we surfaced, my lungs felt ready to burst. On the second ride, I swam in between the dolphins and inhaled deeply before gripping one of each of their pectoral fins. Underwater we went again. We traveled so fast to the far side of the pool, I felt the skin on my face pulling back.

The skin on the dolphins' noses was pink, the gray top layer having rubbed off. Later, when pushed under my feet on a boogie board by two dolphins, I realized how their skin had become damaged. I wondered if it was uncomfortable or if they resented this.

After each activity, the trainers tossed fish into the dolphins' mouths. What I remember most about the experience is that blissful, I could sing out loud, feeling that prevailed the entire time. Maybe Nala and Maya were going through the motions, just doing their jobs, but they never projected that impression.

Since then, I often wonder if one day my wild dolphin friends will invite me to get that close. I would never force it upon them or touch them unless they drifted toward my hand. The experiences I have with them is amazing already. I'm so grateful they feel safe enough around me to spend as much time near me as they do.

Some U.S. federal laws, including the Marine Mammals Protection Act (MMPA) and the Animal Welfare Act (AWA), have been enacted to protect marine species from some of the perils of captivity and transport. In many other countries, though, brutal treatment of dolphins and other marine mammals persists.

I've touched a dolphin only one other time since that life-changing water experience with Nala and Maya in Nuevo Vallarta. Out in my kayak, I spotted a dolphin floating in the water, barely moving. *Is it dead? Or badly injured?* I paddled closer and heard a jerky, wheezing sound whenever she exhaled through her blowhole. Closer observation indicated she was too injured or sick to dive underwater. Her back had bubbled up in angry welts from sun exposure. I spotted linear white gouges along her tail—a chunk of one fluke was missing. Maybe a shark had attacked her?

Could she be saved? I watched for a while, unsure what to do. Then I paddled back to shore and contacted one of the principals from CRRIFS. After Elsa arrived to evaluate the situation, she decided euthanizing the dolphin was the only humane solution. Since the dolphin trusted me, I swam out and gently urged her toward shore.

A kind man from Los Angeles named David had walked back with me after I'd contacted Elsa and her husband. Four of us worked together to drag the injured dolphin from the shallows onto the beach.

A piece of flesh was missing from one of her flukes and claw-like gouges marred the back of her body and what was left of her tail. The dolphin with a blunt rostrum was a Risso's dolphin, Elsa said. She said she believed the dolphin had been attacked by a school of orcas, usually found in deep Sea of Cortez waters well offshore. Orcas often surround one dolphin from the outliers of a pod and then bat it around like a toy, torturing instead of killing it. Then they leave the mortally-wounded dolphin alone in the open sea to die a slow, agonizing death.

David and I comforted the dolphin while Elsa administered the shot. I stroked the dolphin gently and spoke to her. Her skin felt smooth and rubbery. Her eyes were wide and dark. She looked at us with such intentness. She must have wondered why we had removed her from the water. I hoped she could forgive me for gaining her trust and then urging her toward shore to die. We all knew her suffering must have been tremendous. This body she resided in had no life left to give her. We all wanted her to experience peace.

Unfortunately, she batted her flukes onto the sand repeatedly after the first injection. It must have caused panic, pain, or both. This didn't stop until a second shot was administered. I later learned through online research that the injection—the needle inserted into the heart—causes extreme pain and is also difficult to do effectively because of the thick layer of blubber protecting this vital organ.

Finally, the poor dolphin melted into peaceful oblivion. Tears streamed down my cheeks. Watching her suffer had made my chest hurt. I prayed the dolphin felt a sense of peace now and had been ushered into a new world where she was gracefully swimming in a calm sea.

A later necropsy revealed extensive bleeding of her internal organs, including the spleen. The poor creature likely suffered for days, bruised and battered as the waves slowly rolled her toward shore.

CHAPTER TWENTY-FIVE

Mykonos, Greece – October 2016

"More likely their goal was to enrich their whole society, and undeniably, what the Minoans appeared to value most were unquantifiable things like joy and freedom — and dolphins."
Susan Casey – *Voices in the Ocean*

Weeks after returning to the States, the sense of balance I'd found swimming and practicing yoga on Big Corn Island had drained away. I often acted selfishly and felt restless and dissatisfied. I reminded myself that I had a successful career and a happy marriage with the most understanding man in the world. I knew I had rediscovered joy in swimming but was now far away from the sea I adored. I had found a Divine connection out in nature, but back in Tucson, that loving connection was ebbing away.

I signed up for a Yoga Trade membership to search for yoga teaching opportunities in different countries. It opened the possibility of another escape to a faraway place. Within days, I received an offer to teach yoga for three weeks on Mykonos Island, Greece.

Chris and I had visited Crete for a week the previous year before embarking on a swimming vacation around islands in the Ionian Sea. While staying near Heraklion, we walked through the ruins of the famous Knossos Palace, once the ceremonial and political center for the Minoan civilization. Volcanic eruptions, earthquakes, and war eventually annihilated the Minoan people. Their fascination with dolphins is preserved in the colorful frescoes in the Queen's Megaron at Knossos and sites on Santorini Island.

I saw painted dolphins on fresco walls, but not once did I see a live one during our Ionian Sea swims. Maybe I'd see them in Mykonos, I thought, as I composed an email accepting the offer for the yoga position. I had just earned another ticket out of the United States.

The resort sat on a rocky hilltop overlooking Mykonos Town and the brilliant blue waters of the Aegean Sea. The owner, Sharon, offered me a room facing the sea and free breakfasts in exchange for teaching. From my patio, I watched cruise ships arrive and leave the port. The island was beautiful and desolate at the same time. In the distance, the islands of Delos and Tinos projected from the sea. The landscape was barren and trash-littered and often at night a fierce howling wind reminded me I was far from home. The non-potable water running from the tap had to be boated in. The island was a block of rock with no water sources. Bleached white buildings stood out on the rocky landscape. Streets were lined with stone walls.

The town was a labyrinth of corridors. Pirates lost their way trying to navigate through them (the intention when they were built) and so did I. My convoluted meanderings felt like a metaphor for my life. I felt lost in more ways than one when I wandered the stone-paved roads alone, surrounded by channels of white walls, seeing skinny stretches of azure sky overhead. A sign in a store window said *Happiness is not a destination. It's a way of life*.

Yeah, right. It wasn't a way of life for me, and that was the problem. Three months ago, I'd gone to Nicaragua to earn a yoga certification and reconnect with the water. I'd accomplished both of those objectives. Instead of returning home to my ever-supportive husband and applying what I'd learned, I'd felt this overwhelming compulsion to run away again. And now I'd landed on Mykonos where I could swim in the sea every day again, which was nice. But was I any closer to acquiring permanent contentment?

Sattva is the most elevated of the three *gunas* or modes of existence according to yogic philosophy. Associated with happiness, *sattva* is a state of balance, harmony, goodness, purity, and serenity. People exhibit varying proportions of *sattva*, along with the baser qualities of *rajas* and *tamas*. *Tamas* is characterized by disorder, chaos, anxiety, violence, and ignorance. Today's distracted way of living seems to magnify this unbalanced state of mind. Practicing yoga, eating healthily and/or following a spiritual pathway can enhance happiness and the *sattvic* state of existence.

In *Science and Health* (pp. 115-116), Mary Baker Eddy also described three states of being: physical, moral, and spiritual, with spiritual being the most advanced state where an individual expresses wisdom, purity, spiritual understanding, spiritual power, love, health, and holiness.

After more years of living a yogic and Christian lifestyle, I have learned that what I allow into my consciousness and how I live and direct my efforts affects my happiness much more than any physical place or set of material conditions, which are what I turned to for contentment most of my life. Trusting God's guidance, instead of making decisions based on fear, has also been a crucial step for me. It is a journey, though, and for me, that journey has been far from a straight path.

Sharon had hired another volunteer yoga instructor, Debbie from Ohio. One night the three of us ate dinner at a restaurant with a lovely outdoor deck overlooking the water. Another day, we boarded a ferry to Delos and explored the ancient ruins. I spent most of the rest of the time alone.

Debbie spent her free time writing a yoga teacher training manual. In 2017, she visited me in San Carlos and she now owns a yoga retreat center in Uvita, Costa Rica called I Love Yoga Maya. Sharon was occupied with resort management and animal rescue activities. I spent my down time reading, wandering around town, and swimming.

I'd descend the steep trail and thousands of steps into Mykonos Town for a swim or to board a bus bound for one of the other beaches. I always enjoyed that walk because I'd pass a section of dirt road that was particularly unpleasant—lined with two non-working washing machines and other dumped junk—and then all at once, the crescent of beach and endless stretch of cerulean blue water would appear. I never tired of that sudden view of perfect sea. It made me long to run the rest of the way down to the shore, which I might have done if there wasn't such a dire risk of turning an ankle. There were still many steps to descend past adjacent apartments, where I'd see women draping wet clothes over chairs and lines on their balconies, men outside sipping coffee in their underwear. Modesty wasn't popular on this Greek island. On the beach, women routinely changed in and out of swimsuits without much worry over what nude parts might be seen.

I found beauty and companionship in the Aegean Sea. The view of the sea from each beach I visited presented me with different shades of blue and green. In addition to the Mykonos Town Beach I walked to, I visited Platos Gialos, Ornos, and Super Paradise beaches. I could see different Cyclades islands from every beach. Naxos and Delos and Tinos and Paros. I grew lonely walking around and taking the bus everywhere, unable to speak more than a few words of Greek.

I enjoyed my second week the most. I'd overcome my jet lag, the days were still warm and sunny, cruise ship visitors walked the streets, and there were hotel guests to teach in both morning and evening classes.

My third week, Debbie boarded a ferry to Athens and flew back to Ohio. Days later, Sharon flew to England. She said I could leave early if I wanted, but it would have cost more than a thousand dollars for me to change my ticket. Tourist season had ended, most of the tourists had left the island, and the hotel was devoid of guests. Once Sharon left, I was completely alone. She gave me her husband's phone number in case of any emergency.

The first night after everyone had left, a cold front rolled in and wind howled all night. The wind continued all week and temperatures plunged. The sea water turned icy. I intentionally planned daily activities to reduce the sense of loneliness that began to grip me. I took a bus to Platos Gialos beach and got so cold after swimming, I shivered my shoulders into knots during the bus trip back to town.

The next time I returned to that beach, I walked into a restaurant post-swim and ordered lunch so that I could use the bathroom to change into dry clothes. The waiter was studying in Athens and spoke English and I delighted in the few minutes of small talk we exchanged.

As the week rolled on, restaurants closed, and cruise ships stopped coming to the harbor. Streets were deserted, and I had no one to talk to. After three days of not speaking to a single human, I found myself unable to sleep at night.

Many elderly local people continued to come to Mykonos Town beach. None of them could really swim. They would wade, tread water, or swim a slow breaststroke. One woman tried to speak to me one morning, but we simply couldn't communicate. It was so frustrating. Maybe she was trying to tell me that afternoons were less windy at the beach. I'd visited mostly Spanish-speaking countries before where I could speak the language. Thailand and the Czech Republic were the only other countries I'd ever visited where communication was so difficult. And I hadn't traveled alone to either of those places.

The inability to communicate made me feel even more isolated. I became so homesick each day became like an endurance contest. Four more days. Three more days. How the hell would I make it through?

One day I took the bus to Super Paradise Beach and drank two Mai Tais to drown my loneliness. The drinks were ridiculously strong. I knew I shouldn't have had more than one. But temporarily, I felt numb. I could appreciate the beauty of the blue-green sea and the sun sparkling like enormous diamonds on the surface of the water. I'm okay, I told myself until an assaulting headache told me otherwise.

On the bus ride back to Mykonos Town, an older British man engaged me in conversation. He was tall, rail thin, and wore khaki pants and a threadbare plaid shirt. The globalists were conspiring to control the population and take over the world, he said. That's why I needed to vote for Trump.

I didn't really want to talk to him. But I did anyway because he spoke English and I'd been feeling like if I didn't talk to someone soon, I might lose my mind. He invited me to take a ferry with him to Ikaria, an island full of centenarians. In a way I did want to go — not with him, but to experience a new setting.

166

I could book a room at a hotel filled with people instead of staying on at this place, which was silent and dark as a graveyard at night.

Nevertheless, I declined and returned to my room with a full-blown migraine. I popped pills but ended up sick for three days. Every morning I staggered into the kitchen groggy and exhausted, eating what remained of the bread, hard-boiled eggs, and yogurt that were supposed to be my remaining breakfasts.

At home, alone meant an opportunity for relaxation and silence. Here, it felt like torture. Maybe I wasn't an introvert after all. Maybe people really did need to connect with others to survive. At night I heard the walls creak and wind rattling the windows. As I lay awake sobbing, I wished I could be stronger. How could one week of isolation push me over a cliff into emotional break down?

I tried reading Harry Potter books on my Kindle. I'd immersed myself in them many times before when I needed escape. But I'd read two lines and lose track of what was happening. At night, I tried listening to relaxing music or Yoga Nidra sequences. None of those helped me sleep. I felt like I'd had three cups of coffee. I trembled all night with anxiety.

I never slept a full night until after I left Mykonos. I ran outside early the morning of my return flight with my suitcases, paranoid the cab wouldn't come or one of my flights would be cancelled. I knew one thing for sure. No matter what happened, I would not return to that hotel. I couldn't sleep in that room for another night. Fortunately, I returned home without incident.

We're basically social creatures. And dolphins are even more than we are. Thinking back on this experience, I often wonder if dolphins experience this on-the-brink-of-insanity kind of loneliness when they are stolen away from their home waters and loving families and tossed alone into an unfamiliar pool. What does night after night alone feel like to them?

I had booked another Yoga Trade trip to Ecuador, but I promptly canceled it. There were worse things than being in the United States, such as being completely isolated in a strange place. I wanted to be home, with my husband and my children—now grown but still living with us. I would fall asleep on my husband's shoulder like I did every night at home. And Marion and I could go take a yoga class at Miraval together on a day off. And we'd all go to Catalina State Park one weekend to hike the trails. I loved my family so much and being apart from them had made sense for the yoga teacher training, but not for something like this. Location mattered, sure. But family mattered more.

CHAPTER TWENTY-SIX

February 2019 – San Carlos, México

"There's no question dolphins are smarter than humans as
they play more."
– Albert Einstein

One overcast February morning, laminated layers of clouds
masked the rising sun. From the beach, I spotted dolphins just
offshore and sprinted toward the water, calling out, "Wait for
me." Some days they're still near me by the time I swim out,
other days they're already a half a mile down the shoreline.
They don't always breach the surface on a regular interval.
Sometimes, they stay under water for long periods of time—if
they want to avoid boats and Jet Skis or even swimmers. While
humans breathe involuntarily, dolphins must make a conscious
choice to breathe through the blowholes on top of their heads

whenever they surface. The interval between breaths might last only seconds or it can be as long as 15 minutes.

I've often seen the dolphins moving sluggishly, seemingly drifting along the surface of the water. A chapter in *The Dolphin in the Mirror* leads me to believe this dolphin lethargy is sleep. Dolphins, like humans, have two brain hemispheres. While both of our hemispheres descend into unconsciousness when we sleep, dolphins don't have that luxury.

One hemisphere of the dolphin brain must remain active in order to breathe and watch for predators. While one side sleeps, the other side takes the driver's seat. Dolphins take intermittent naps on and off throughout the day and night to rest. I wonder if my dolphin friends get sufficient rest when boats are constantly chasing them?

Although dolphins are colorblind, they are very sensitive to light in the blue wavelengths, ideal for their watery world. Since the dolphin eye has more rod cells than the human eye, it is hypersensitive to low-light conditions encountered at depth. They can see clearly even in dim light. While humans must wear goggles to see underwater, dolphins have sharp vision in and out of the water.

During San Carlos winters, the Sea of Cortez temperatures plummet to the upper 50s and low 60s Fahrenheit. My dolphin-look-a-like-suit is mandatory in this kind of cold. Dolphins have no need of a wetsuit, since they have an insulated layer of blubber around their bodies to keep them warm.

Visibility that morning was poor, so I heard a whistle before a dark shape appeared underneath me. I imagine the lead dolphin's whistle was his warning to the others that a human had been spotted at one o'clock. Or maybe the call helped them place me in space. A moment later, the dolphin's white beak or rostrum glided by so close, I could have touched it.

Another morning, the rising sun had painted Tetakawi and the other rocky volcanic slopes to the west a brilliant pink. A supermoon—where the full moon appears larger and more luminescent than normal because it is closer to Earth—slowly descended toward the jagged mountain peaks. Despite all this beauty, the dolphins captured most of my attention. They leaped from the water at regular intervals—one in front of the other—moving at a rapid pace. They leaped, their powerful, wet bodies ignited orange by the rising sun. They leaped so close to their companions in this long line, so powerful and graceful, without a single collision. I'm not sure if there was a reason for their unusual energy. Maybe the supermoon keyed them up. Or an especially tasty fish meal had energized them.

I've been around the dolphins in San Carlos enough to see them working as a team. A lead dolphin watches for danger and talks via whistles, squeaks, and clicks—maybe for echolocation and communicating with others. Behind the pack, another security guard dolphin appears keenly aware. Moms and babies swim so close—as if their bodies are connected—and often surface simultaneously. The dolphins zoom fast when chasing schools of fish. Sometimes, they stun fish by slapping them with their tails or flukes. I've seen them work in tandem with pelicans, a group of them "herding" the fish for the benefit of the pelicans and themselves.

When their schedule permits, they take time out to play. On days when large swells rise and fall near the shore, the dolphins body surf. Happy hour can take place in the morning as readily as any other time. I've watched them pass pufferfish to each other. This same fish, which is toxic or even fatal to humans, apparently gives dolphins a high—it's a chew toy with a buzz. I wonder if they, like so many of the human species, get addicted to substances. Or can they ride on the pleasure train occasionally and then disembark without consequences?

Diana Reiss discusses the complexities of dolphin relationships in *The Dolphin in the Mirror*. The research she shares demonstrates that dolphins are self-aware and adaptable. They can go with the flow in changing circumstances. The dolphins I know play in boat wakes and entertain audiences by leaping from the water and turning flips. Once, after a tropical storm, where a day ago, the sea had been a foaming, tumultuous angry mass of enormous waves, the pod glided along the coastline chasing fish as if the storm never happened.

The dolphins often interact with me near the mouth of the El Soldado Estuary. Hide and seek is one favorite game. A dorsal fin appears, then slips beneath the surface of the water again. And the next thing I know, the teasing dolphin releases a watery exhale right behind me. I've been tricked once again! The dolphins circle around me on their sides or backs or swim close enough to peek at me face-to-face. One of the babies veers near and the mother nudges her away, perhaps warning the youth about the unpredictability of humans.

I hear a squeak, or a series of clicks, and wonder if the dolphins are trying to communicate with me or are speaking to each other. That day, as always, they played gently with me, but rougher with one another. Some of the dolphins zoomed through the water at great speeds, creating large wakes of water. Others leaped into the air and landed with a tremendous splash. I watched one smack the water with his tail and then two engaged in a tail slapping game. But the dolphins never moved fast around me. They seemed to know I'm too fragile for rough play. Or maybe they didn't want to scare me.

Once the dolphins were out of sight, I watched a tern plunge into the water just in front of me, clumsily thrashing around in the water before lifting off with a sardine in its mouth. I swam toward a mass feeding of thousands of pelicans, gulls, terns, boobies, and cormorants. I attempted to quietly swim breaststroke further from shore around them in hopes they wouldn't take much notice of me. All at once, hundreds of panicked birds squawked and flew into the air, blocking most of the sunlight.

So much for me trying to blend in with the waves and the water. I felt sad. One human in the water and I'd caused so much chaos. At least next time I'd know to swim the same way the bird mob was traveling. Chalk it up to one more new and unique experience out in the wild sea.

CHAPTER TWENTY-SEVEN

Grand Cayman Island - April 2017

The second month into my leave of absence from work my daughter and I took a ten-day trip to Grand Cayman. We left Tucson early and didn't land on the island until late at night. We were delayed leaving Florida because the flight attendants had to clear customs and there was another wait for the maintenance logbook to be signed. The flight south was short, but we had to circle the island more than once before landing due to dogs on the runway.

We rolled our suitcases through a construction zone across the street to the strip of rental car offices. It was a balmy evening—humid and warm, with a lovely breeze. Fortunately, the Avis office was deserted of other travelers. Within minutes we had finished the paperwork and were in the car. Driving on the left side of the road—something I'd never done before—was scary. My seat was on the right, as was the handle for the turn signals. I kept flipping on the wind shield wipers by mistake whenever attempting to signal.

My GPS wasn't working and the written directions I had to the Turtle Nest Inn didn't make much sense to me. I quickly got lost in the maze of streets and industrial complexes near the airport. I pulled off into a parking lot to debate about what to do next. A van pulled up behind us and a man stepped out of the vehicle and approached. Was he a police officer? Someone who wanted to rob us? I anxiously rolled down the window.

Speaking in English, the man explained that he was a taxi driver. He asked where we were going and when I named the place we'd booked in Bodden Town, he said he lived in that community, knew the way to the inn, and asked us to follow him. My stress melted away. He drove just in front of us the whole way, slowing down with flashing lights next to our hotel. I offered him a tip and a thank you, and minutes later, we checked into our room.

The second-floor seaside apartment had two balconies, a kitchen, bedroom, and bathroom. The kitchen cupboards were painted brilliant white to match the white tile floors. Brightly-colored Caribbean style furniture accented the apartment. Orange sofas surrounded a white bamboo coffee table in the living area and the white-painted bamboo chairs, arranged around a round glass kitchen table, had cushions patterned in blue, yellow, and orange. We pulled open the sliding doors to hear the sound of the waves. Every night, we opened the sliding door, so we could fall asleep listening to the soothing sigh of the Caribbean Sea.

During the night, I dreamed about swimming. Maybe because I heard the sound of waves even deep in sleep and could smell and taste the salt in the air. I couldn't wait to swim. And as soon as the sun arose, I ran out the door. On purpose, I'd booked this family resort far removed from the high-rise hotels, where a huge reef rife with sea life followed the contours of the shore. I wasn't interested in Jet Skis and paddleboards. I wanted a place I could snorkel and swim for hours.

The seas were rough but there weren't any dangerous currents inside of the reef. I waded through thick patches of waving seagrass before reaching water deep enough to swim in. Colorful fish darted around as I swam along, relishing the soothing warmth of the Caribbean waters.

Before my swim, when the first pale light illuminated our Grand Cayman room, I gazed at my daughter's face and noticed how beautiful and calm she looks sleeping. Her eyelashes are as long as they were when she was a baby. Her smooth skin glows, her heart-shaped face looks childlike and innocent—in her slumber she appears to be in a state of complete contentment and peace. She's not wondering why her ex-boyfriend of four years is with a 19-year-old woman less than a month after they broke up. She's not worried about how she will manage her nursing school schedule.

For weeks, I'd looked forward to this trip, to this opportunity to spend quality time with her, which didn't happen often enough. One day soon she would move away, find her own apartment, and I'd regret those missed opportunities, those days we might have connected when the time was lost to a migraine or some other task or project that then seemed important.

It turned out to be a wonderful week of bonding—there were outings, trips to the grocery store, chats in the pool or on the beach, meals prepared together to savor out on our balcony along with a glass of wine.

A few times we visited Spotts Beach—which was only about two miles from our Turtle Nest Inn. I'd park along the road across the street. We had to run for it to cross since there was a steady stream of traffic. Squawking chickens welcomed us to the beach. Beautiful turquoise water beckoned and within minutes we were swimming through crystal clear water, gazing at fish and green sea turtles feasting on waving fields of sea grass. Silver tags pierced many of their flippers.

Each day, we swam by adult green turtles and many smaller juveniles. Full grown adults weigh as much as 485 pounds. I loved watching these magnificent creatures flap their flippers, flying gracefully through the water. Whenever they surfaced for a bite of air, I admired their hooked beaks and the lizard-like scales crowning their heads—above water, they looked like blocky brown-orange puzzle pieces with green spaces in between.

Female green turtles nest up to seven times in a season. Although the green turtle is listed as a threatened species under the U.S. Endangered Species Act and is protected, sadly, sea turtles are still hunted in Grand Cayman and many other countries.

One afternoon late in the week, we signed up to have Captain Dexter boat us and some other tourists out to a shallow place in the sea to pet and play with dozens of enormous Southern stingrays in crystal clear water. Dexter, a wiry, tanned elderly man, had survived throat cancer, and had nursed one badly injured stingray back into health. He and his partner, Amos, fed the stingrays squid, and the enormous creatures— some five feet in diameter—acted downright affectionate with them, bouncing around in the water and nuzzling up against their bodies.

After having witnessed my husband and stepson suffer painful wounds inflicted by stingrays, I never imagined I'd feel friendly toward one, let alone allow one to give me a rubbery back rub. But the buoyant personalities of the stingrays really moved me.

Another afternoon, we strolled through nearby botanical gardens and learned the names of dozens of tropical trees. I was shocked to see a birch tree in this tropical place when the only birch I'd seen before was the white variety in northern Michigan. We spotted two blue iguanas in the breeding area. They were enormous, with saggy throats and scaly faces. Their horned eyelids and pouting expressions suggested they wouldn't hesitate to bite. They changed color with their environment much like the green iguana, which isn't protected or native to the island, but can uniquely swim and climb trees.

Late in the week, we visited Starfish Beach. We peacefully snorkeled in the shallows, gazing through our masks at hundreds of orange brittle starfish nestled in the sea grass. Then the crowds arrived. Children kicked sand in our faces and ran into the water, stirring up sediment and decimating the plant life. We grabbed our towels and moved to a quieter part of the beach. We went for another swim and by then there were so many Jet Skis and boats around, we gave up and headed to Rum Point for lunch.

Sitting at a picnic table under a fir tree, Marion dined on Jerked Chicken while I feasted on a cheeseburger. The place was too touristy for my taste, and I was relieved to return to the quiet haven of Turtle Nest Inn.

Owners Duane and Marlene, originally from Ontario, Canada, had moved to Grand Cayman 20 years earlier and built their inn from the ground up. What a gift their place was. Every morning, we woke to hear the sea—along with the cock-a-doodle-doo of roosters greeting the dawn. I often wondered if the locals ate any of the chickens that ran wild all over the island. We saw and heard them everywhere except in the swanky resort areas.

Marion occasionally became quiet or burst into tears since the breakup with her boyfriend had happened so recently. It was difficult to see her unhappy and hard to think of the right words to say to comfort her. It was sad to see how this relationship, which had started off with the two of them as best friends and in love, had ended so suddenly and in such a bad way. I had hoped her boyfriend would gain the maturity to settle down permanently, but he had always seemed restless. He changed jobs often, traveled a lot, and now, it seemed, he wanted a different girl. And my daughter was left with a broken heart.

I was present with Marion, not talking too much or only vaguely listening while thinking ahead about what I needed to do next. At least temporarily, I felt in synch with myself, too. I swam in the sea and felt like I'd found truth. What could be better than this? Sitting in a chair by the ocean, digging my toes in the sand underneath a coconut tree while talking to Marion about men and nursing school and trips she'd take one day. Swimming among dozens of stingrays through water clear as crystal. Floating over a sea turtle and watching it dine on sea grass. On that island, I didn't have to tell myself to stop and enjoy my daughter's company. I had all the time in the world to relax and listen and my mind and the world around me wasn't fighting against this plan.

At the airport, we conversed with a petite American woman with light brown hair, cut short and neatly styled. Once she learned that Marion was studying to become a nurse, she told us she had just retired from a long, successful nursing career. It gave me hope—seeing how she seemed undamaged by the hardships of this very challenging profession. She had found her career very rewarding and didn't appear to be hardened by the experience. She radiated warmth and kindness.

During the long flight home, I closed my eyes and saw the ocean behind my eyelids. A sea turtle diving down toward the waving sea grass, millions of tiny minnows shooting through the water under a dock, the undulating crystal-clear water, an orange brittle starfish held in my daughter's hand, just underwater. It was as if all those images became permanently recorded in my brain.

And yet, four days after my return from Grand Cayman, I could no longer see the water behind my eyelids when I closed them.

Stolen away from the soothing sanctuary of the sea, I felt my true self drowned out once again by the rhythms of American life. I felt compelled to hurry, to rush, to achieve. I got caught up in this current and pulled away from what I wanted. To be present in my life. To be grateful for every minute I spent with the people I loved. To feel connected with nature and the outdoors.

I tried to start the day right with a yoga practice. I dragged my mat out in our back yard and started a sequence of poses. But soon the sounds of the birds were blocked out by the sound of a screeching saw. My neighbor was running his construction company out of his house again. Despair washed over me. I'd complained twice to the town, and they'd talk to him, and he'd say he wouldn't do it anymore and then start again a week later. I couldn't do this anymore. I had to run away from America. This time for good.

CHAPTER TWENTY-EIGHT

Puerto Vallarta, México - December 10-13, 2018

I had lived in México for nearly a year and a half. I only returned to the States to visit family and usually stayed for less than a week. Always, I eagerly returned to my daily sea swims, the yoga classes I taught at Bahía Delfín and at a studio in town, following the laid-back rhythm of my new life.

Chris and I flew to Puerto Vallarta for a week-long trip. Our high-rise hotel, the Sunscape, is only one of many tall edifices along the beach amidst the hustle and bustle of the tourist area and far from old town where we had stayed on our previous visit. With dozens of floors and hundreds of rooms, the pool and the lobby areas were overrun with swimsuit-clad bodies slick with sweat and sunscreen. Kids screamed and drunk guests laughed and talked too loudly.

Most guests were there to work on their tans and drink margaritas and *Dos Equis*. Early morning—when most guests were still asleep—was my favorite times to venture out. I'd walk down to the beach for a sea swim or perform sun salutations in the sand, savoring the view of lush green mountains along the curving coastline.

One morning, I took a short sea swim. I stayed within the buoyed-off areas since there was a lot of boat traffic around. I spotted a group of dolphins arcing over the water far in the distance. I floated on the waves, watching them. I thought of my dolphin friends in San Carlos and sent them a silent prayer. In my mind's eye, I could see their smiling faces, their streamlined bodies rocketing through the water, and I imagined I heard their excited squeaks.

I would take a Yoga Nidra workshop with Anna Laurita, the owner of a yoga studio called Davannayoga. Yoga Nidra is a form of guided meditation where the participant stays awake while descending into a deep state of rest and experiences all of his or her five koshas or energetic layers of being. The practice intrigued me, and I wanted to explore it more.

After my swim and breakfast, I walked the three miles from our hotel to Anna's studio instead of taking a bus or taxi. It seemed like too much of a hassle to figure out the logistics and I welcomed the walk anyway, since I anticipated my fidgety body might struggle with long periods of stillness.

I walked past shopping plazas, grocery stores, and gas stations, while trucks and buses and cars roared by. I strolled past a vacant lot. Behind a chain-linked fence, a disintegrating stucco structure was overgrown with bushes and weeds, protected by a security guard. His reason for protecting the place was a mystery to me.

Sweat dripped from my brow by the time I reached the more tranquil *malecón* or coastal walkway. No car traffic was allowed, and an ocean breeze cooled my overheated body. The wide, textured sidewalks along the ocean were accented at street junctions by statues. I walked along, gazing at the ocean and listening to the waves crashing on the shore. When I reached the street I sought, I turned sharply away from the Pacific Ocean, walking inland a couple of blocks before sweating my way up hundreds of stairs. Lushly vegetated trees with climbing vines grew over any exposed earth the stairs and bracketing homes and apartment buildings weren't occupying. I stepped up stairs where red ceramic hearts had been artistically arranged into a mosaic in the cement.

Anna's studio was on a street corner, I discovered, as I stood breathless and panting after climbing what seemed like thousands of stairs. A sign on the house door indicated a class was in session. Another student, a tall, fair-skinned Canadian named Kirby, stood outside waiting. He looked to be in his early thirties. His dark hair was cropped close to his scalp on top and on the sides with just one little curly trail of hair left to grow wild at the nape of his neck.

A few minutes later, Anna invited us inside the studio—a room of her house converted into a yoga space. The floors were ceramic tile and with the windows open to the street, the din of cars and street vendors was ushered in.

There were three of us in the class—me, Kirby and a woman named Emily, also from Canada.

I found the Yoga Nidra practices very soothing and relaxing, like the most amazing gift you can give yourself. Descending into the deepest realms of my being and losing track of time felt so freeing. It made me want to give that experience to others, so they could experience the same sense of peace. Often since then, I've practiced in afternoons to refresh myself, or before bed, so I drift off into a relaxed sleep.

Twice during lunch breaks, Kirby and I walked to a nearby restaurant for a buffet vegetarian lunch. He talked about the business he had started up with his former (male) romantic partner. He mentioned that his body wasn't amenable to vegetarianism. He said he'd read that the energy would be ideal for him to be in Puerto Vallarta—so he'd decided to live there for the winter to practice and teach yoga. But he worried he wouldn't be able to teach.

Kirby said he was easily distracted and couldn't remember information he'd just studied or read about. Clearly, he lacked confidence. It felt strange to be in my 50s, looking back and trying to recall myself more than 30 years ago—about to teach my first fitness classes—so I could put his concerns in perspective and respond appropriately. Now, I taught classes intuitively—seeing who showed up and pulling from memory whatever would work best for that particular set of students.

I shared stories about my early days teaching fitness classes. I told him how sometimes I would practice for two hours in preparation for just one class. If some small condition went awry, like a cassette tape getting chewed up, it would throw off my whole class. In the beginning, it was hard to adapt to glitches. I had nightmares about forgetting my music, or the equipment being broken, or my mind going blank in the middle of a dance sequence.

But I said, every year of teaching would cement his knowledge until eventually, teaching would come very naturally. Until then, he would have to do lots of prep. I told him swimming before a class sent me into the room feeling grounded and centered. Maybe he could establish that pre-class mental state through a regular yoga and meditation practice.

I told him I thought he was amazing because he is real and honest. I think he took what I shared to heart. I often wonder if Kirby's continued to spend winters in Puerto Vallarta and if he's teaching now.

I love people like Kirby. People who speak the truth and aren't afraid to hear it from another make me feel all warm and cozy inside. For a little while, I can let my guard down, and just be who I am. Kirby's open, understanding demeanor was like a light that compelled me to walk toward it.

CHAPTER TWENTY-NINE

San Carlos, México – February 2019

The Color Run would start near the Marina Terra hotel. My husband had signed up. I wasn't in running shape, so I planned to watch. We weren't sure where to go the day of the race. When Chris had registered, the woman who collected the money had told us the start would be *cerca de aquí* which meant nearby.

We weren't all that surprised by the uncertainty. It's pretty much normal for México. Either the registrar didn't know, or the race start location hadn't been decided yet. We figured we'd drive around the area in the morning until we encountered banners and a crowd. Sure enough, a dusty parking lot near the Palapa Griega was filling with cars and a crowd had gathered around an orange and white inflatable start/finish line arch.

After parking, the next obstacle was to obtain Chris's timing chip and number. We asked around. A man said he had picked his stuff up in Guaymas. The details of what we should do, explained in rapid fire Spanish, remained foggy to us.

We joined a long line of people. Chris received a shirt and his special sunglasses to protect his eyes when people threw the colored chalk at him, but no number or chip. We had to see someone else for that, the woman said. Another man we asked told us to stand next to a woman with a stroller. They were making more chips and would bring the number and chip to Chris if we waited beside her.

We ran into a Canadian couple from Bahía Delfín, Bob and Janice. Both of them wanted to do the race. Neither had registered. Naturally, they hoped we had some clue. We told them what we knew. Twenty minutes later, someone brought a number and a chip to Chris. Janice eventually got a chip, but Bob didn't. He didn't mind too much. I'm not in running shape anyway, he said.

The event was designed with family fun in mind. Whole families ran together—moms, dads, bunches of kids. Even aunts and uncles and neighbors. All the registrants were given a bag of powdered, colored chalk. Chalk flew everywhere even before the race began. I burst out laughing more than once. Faces turned shades of blue, pink, purple, and orange. The air became a cloud of color.

Two young girls walked past us, picking up discarded plastic bottles and tossing them into a trash bag held by their mother. I smiled and felt a burst of joy and hope. Some Mexicans do care about the Earth even though many arrogant Americans say they don't. It is so easy to stereotype people. People who come to the beach to play loud music, drink all night, and throw their trash everywhere aren't representative of the general Mexican attitude.

Kids chased each other around, laughing, throwing colored chalk at friends and family and anyone else who happened to be standing nearby. Chris had left his chalk bag in the car. I told him to get it. In the end, he did — maybe for self-defense. By the time the race started, almost everyone had rainbow colors on their shirts, their faces.

Runners were pelted with colored chalk when the starting gun fired. I heard the stomping of hundreds of feet. Clouds of red, purple, yellow, blue, and orange chalk rose into the air.

I walked to the beach for some solitude and returned to the blaring music and announcer's voice in time to see Chris finish. His shirt, his hair and most of his face were powdered in purple. Chris said race volunteers had been stationed at various intervals along the course, tossing chalk at everyone.

Chris placed first in his age group, but it was a long wait for the awards ceremony. Mexican races are more about fun and celebration than winning. First, there was music and dancing. Then public officials spoke. Chris became increasingly impatient and told me he wanted to leave, but I encouraged him to stay. Finally, the organizers announced his name and he stepped up high on the podium. He shook the second and third place finishers' hands and then the three of them raised their connected hands to the sky in victory.

It was a wonderful sight to see my husband smile. He looked happy for a moment — even in México — standing on a podium with noise and chaos all around him. Maybe being in his comfort zone didn't need to be requisite for joy. It no longer was for me.

Instead of a medal, he received a canvas bag of goodies from the Ponto sardine company. We had to laugh out loud when we looked inside. He had been gifted several cans of sardines, an apron, and a tortilla warmer. Although this form of award seemed odd to us, it makes sense to offer winners prizes they can use instead of more medals to throw in a drawer and forget about.

A year later in March of 2020, I'd run this same Color Run with my friends José and Mercedes and win my age group while Chris remained in Tucson, happy to have a break from México. I threw chalk at people and laughed and put tissue in my ears to drown out the loud music.

I anticipated competing in the Kino Bay and Miramar swims next, but the Color Run would be my last race on land or in the water in 2020. Days later, the COVID-19 pandemic became a crisis in North America. The 2020 Color Run was the last hurrah before social distancing and fear and isolation took over.

CHAPTER THIRTY

San Carlos, México – April 2019

Huge crowds flood the beaches during *Semana Santa* — the week of Easter. We were told that we had to acquire a pass from the San Carlos police station if we wanted to drive into town that week. Roads became so clogged with cars, it could take more than four hours to get to town and back. I decided to shop on Monday and not use the truck the rest of the week. I'd hunker down and observe the mounting chaos from the safety of our condo and San Francisco Beach.

On Monday, the beach was still deserted, and I enjoyed a delightful swim in the sea, watching flocks of cormorants soar over me while I stroked through the salty blue water. Tuesday turned out to be a quiet, nearly normal April beach day. On Wednesday, tents popped up on the beach. One person stuck a pole with a Mexican flag into the sand, which blew in the breeze — a symbol of this tradition of families gathering on the beach.

As tents advanced from a scattered few to covering most visible stretches of sand, I felt increasingly lonely. I would spend this religious holiday in isolation. Most of my friends had headed north and my husband wouldn't return until after our upcoming home closing.

We were about to simplify our lives and move into a smaller, easier-to-care-for Tucson house. We'd sold the furniture we no longer wanted on Craigslist. I'd been in Tucson to help Chris box up stuff for the big move that would happen at the end of April. He was finishing up more work while I had returned to México for a short reprieve.

People camped in Coleman tents and under shade canopies or had even constructed ad-hoc tents from cardboard and fabric or beach towels. Some created tent cities for their families and friends in arcs or circles. I tried not to think of how toileting was being handled, although as the week marched on, the foul odor on the breeze delivered an unpleasant clue.

Seeing so many Mexicans surrounded by their loved ones made me feel isolated. My husband, Chris, was in Tucson, my two children were in Tucson, my mom was in Tucson. Six hours in the car and I could be with them, but it felt like a vast ocean separated us.

In a month, we'd enjoy views of the rocky, cactus-decorated Tortolita Mountains from our new back yard when we weren't in San Carlos savoring views of the blue-green sea. Chris planned to spend more time in Tucson while I planned to spend most of the year in México, where I'd met new friends and become absorbed in sea turtle rescue work and yoga teaching.

Families seated in chairs faced the water, drinks in hand. Children laughed and chased each other, scattering sand everywhere, or they crouched in the sand, digging, and building castles and sculpting animal shapes, decorating them with shells.

It had been decades since I had knelt in the white sands of Clearwater Beach, Florida with my brother, Dave, constructing shapes with mounds of sand. All the tents grouped together reminded me of camping trips to West Virginia I once took with my mom, dad, and brother when I was seven, eight, nine maybe. It had been fun to catch minnows in the stream with Dave and swim in the lake with my Yogi Bear floatie toy, but it had always just been the four of us in the mountains — we were never surrounded by cousins, aunts, uncles, or grandparents. We saw my grandparents on trips to Florida, and my aunt and uncle during the two weeks we traveled by train to New Brunswick, Canada every summer.

I wonder if anyone feels lonely in México. I've rarely seen a Mexican national alone here. No one sitting alone at a restaurant table, reading a book alone under a beach umbrella, walking alone on the beach. Even the poorest of people — street performers that juggle, ride unicycles or breathe fire, people selling candy or washing windshields — tend to travel in groups. And on the beach, I often see families of five, six, or even 20 or more.

Every evening that week, I walked up and down San Francisco Beach, watching families of all generations enjoying each other's company. Mamás were busy building sandwiches, papás were grilling burgers, grandmothers gratefully received a drink carefully passed by a child.

People drank beer or soda, laughing and talking. A young boy waded into the sea wearing his pajamas. The row of wooden posts used to keep SUVs from entering the area in front of Bahía Delfín now had a long line of rope connected to it. Clothes, towels, and swimsuits hung from this newly assembled clothesline, swinging in the breeze.

Some families had brought kayaks and rafts to the beach. Those new to the sport paddled awkwardly in the choppy afternoon waves. The tent city was always silent in the early morning, with almost everyone still fast asleep. The seas then tended to be calm as a mill pond.

One night when the water was smooth as glass, I paddled offshore on my paddleboard. People watched me curiously. Two kids shouted to me. I waved back at them.

I have witnessed many Mexican celebrations on the beach since this night. At a baby gender reveal one summer, I babysat an injured pelican while rockets shot sparks and clouds of blue powder exploded all around me. Always there are big groups of Mexicans, always celebrations are loud and with everyone drinking excessive amounts of alcohol. Breathing deep to stay calm, I prayed for the bird, and she eventually flew off into the night.

Trash began to accumulate. That Friday night, I carried a large trash bag during my walk, picking up cans, bottles, and all sorts of plastic and Styrofoam. A drunk man whistled to me, then ordered me to collect beer cans from his entire group. His surly command offended me, but I wasn't in the mood to fight. I collected the trash, internally boiling inside, irritated that some people thought it was okay to leave their garbage on the beach, that they had no respect for the beauty of their surroundings or the wildlife that fought so hard to survive, so often disrupted by human activity.

I respected that people wanted to spend the Easter holiday with family and friends. But what made little sense to me is that most of these celebrations led to intoxication—another shot of tequila, another six beers—and ultimately a mindlessly discarded trail of trash. I honestly have no respect for drunkenness or the disorder that it leads to—regardless of what country you're from.

By Sunday morning's swim, most of the temporary tent city had disappeared. Maybe people had gone to Catholic mass — to make amends for all the partying — or were driving home to Hermosillo, Ciudad Obregón, and Nogales. Their departure allowed the creatures living in the sea, estuary, and dunes and desert to return to a state of harmony.

A neighbor invited me to attend a community church service. I accepted the invitation because I craved company and going to church was a way to honor God and Jesus's teachings and resurrection. I hadn't attended a service in months since there aren't any Christian Science churches in San Carlos. They hadn't yet begun offering the Zoom services they began and have continued since the pandemic.

I found the church service depressing. The pastor's sermon emphasized the suffering of Jesus's crucifixion instead of the miracle of his resurrection, which was always the focus of our Easter services. It was a monumental accomplishment, overcoming death, I thought. So why wasn't this pastor focusing on that? It was the whole purpose of Jesus being on Earth, I thought, to show mankind that material laws that say we're doomed to sin, sickness, and death are merely an illusion and that our spiritual identities — as created by God — can be discovered and are immune from destruction.

The pastor then warned us that in every marriage, one spouse would die first, as if to put the final nail in the coffin, literally, and to make sure everyone in attendance would leave the service with the wind knocked out of them. I wondered why anyone would want to attend a service like this. Many churches seemed determined to hammer guilt and fear into peoples' consciousnesses and I'd always wondered why. How does that help anyone? Could this be one reason why church attendance is rapidly declining worldwide? People need hope, to be lifted and brought closer to God, not to be further beaten down with discouraging words.

So many churches preach that their denomination's path is the only right one. So many wars have been fought over religion. So many people have died, who could have lived. In I John, it says, "Beloved, let us love one another: for love is of God; and every one that loveth is born of God, and knoweth God."

To me, the instructions in this passage of the Bible are so simple. God wants us to love others more than anything else. God wanted us to be unified rather than divided. And in so many cases, instead of following this precept, humans choose to judge, condemn, and exclude—even to inflict violence on others who don't share their beliefs.

My spiritual journey involves seeking inspiration and then finding the right way to convey it to others—whether it's by leading a yoga practice or meditation, sharing information about sea turtles, mentioning a passage from an inspiring book, saying kind words, praying silently for someone, or even gifting someone, who I think will be receptive to it, a copy of *Science and Health*.

That path to sharing what will help and inspire others isn't always easy. Sometimes, I struggle to find the right words or to decide what gift is right to share. I will keep asking God to help me do this better and know that day by day, I will become a better listener. Jesus once said (Matthew 19:26), "with God all things are possible."

CHAPTER THIRTY-ONE

San Carlos and Kino Bay, México – May 18-19, 2019

"En cada brazada escribimos una página en la historia de la natación de Sonora (in each stroke, we write a page in the history of swimming in Sonora)."
– inscription on gold medals from 2019 and 2022 Kino Bay races

My daughter and her friend, Larren, drove down from Tucson to visit. We dined out, strolled to the estuary, and sat on the beach and talked.

It saddened me to see them go at the end of their stay. Although I had to tread carefully—I often tend to say things that annoy Marion—there had been fleeting moments when I felt deeply connected to my daughter. One morning, I had given temple massages to everyone in my yoga class during *savasana*. As I had gently rubbed the smooth soft skin on

Marion's forehead, my fingers damp with lavender essential oil, she had opened her big brown eyes and looked at me, a soft smile on her face. Her big eyelashes had softened her expression even more.

Another day, while the sea breeze ruffled her hair and waves crashed on the sand, she had opened up her heart to me, sharing a traumatic personal situation she was facing, and I had done my best to offer understanding and support.

There were hugs and goodbyes and then I stood and watched Marion's gray Ford Focus round the corner and disappear. Later that morning, Chris and Keith and I would drive to Kino Bay—a nearby seaside town—about a 2.5 hour drive away. I had signed up to do a 1600-meter sea swim race there the next morning.

We drove on Mex 15 for 30 miles and then turned left on 61 at a Pemex gas station. We maneuvered around mounds of dirt to follow the narrow, paved road with unpredictable dips and rises. My heartrate skyrocketed whenever a semi flew past from the other direction. The jagged volcanic landscape flattened out and soon we were surrounded by an endless view of flat, dusty ground. We seemed to be driving to the edge of nowhere. Once we reached the junction with 100, the highway from Hermosillo to Kino Bay, the road conditions improved.

Finding the Posada del Mar—the hotel I'd reserved per the race director's recommendations—wasn't difficult. But the place looked abandoned. Black doors with cracked paint, a cement block structure with rusty rebar sticking out, and broken windows were the predominant features. The three of us looked at each other doubtfully and then stepped into the dreary lobby. The dark, olive stain-glassed windows blocked the light to the point that I felt like I stood inside a cave. I could barely see my feet.

I offered my name to the front desk attendant. Her brows drew together, and she asked if we'd like to see a room. We followed her down the dark hallway. She pushed a creaky door open to reveal two mattresses sitting on concrete blocks, black curtains hanging from a small window that matched the paint and the dark tile on the floor. The place could take a person from manic joy to deep depression in a matter of minutes.

Chris said later it was the worst room he had ever seen, and I had to agree it was right up there with Richie's motel — a dump where I'd stayed with undergraduate classmates at a geology conference in North Carolina — thanks to our geology club President Randy's excessive frugality with our funds.

Beyond the flimsy curtains and saltwater-misted window was the pool. I heard splashing and screaming. The pool was clearly the center of attraction for the place. Music blared from someone's car stereo in the parking lot. Chris gave me a "no way I can stay here" look. I wondered what it would be like to sleep in our car.

The woman gave us the way out we were desperate for. There are other hotels with TVs and views of the ocean, she said. I asked if she would be offended if we cancelled our stay. She said no, it would be fine. We thanked her and dashed out the door.

Driving into town, I'd seen brilliant white stone buildings right on the sea that reminded me of visits to the Greek islands. Those would be great, I said to Keith and Chris. But there were no vacancies. We queried at the office of the Las Toninas hotel where the swim race would start. All full. We drove further into town becoming increasingly agitated when we were unable to find vacant rooms that were even halfway passable. We had previously passed a place called the Sunset Suites. I finally decided to turn around and check out that place. I walked inside the office to inquire about a room and let out a relieved sigh when the attendant said they had one vacancy.

Room number eight was on the second floor. It had numerous oddities, including cracked walls, peeling paint and single bulbs hanging from ceilings, but there was sufficient light and space for the three of us to stay a night without the need for antidepressants. There was also a sitting room and kitchen. Outside our front door was a large common area – a big patio with stone tables and wrought iron chairs. We just had to be careful going into the bathroom because there was a 3-inch step down.

The bedroom had two beds. A sliding door leading to a narrow ledge-like patio, offered an amazing view of the sea. The rocky peaks of Alcatraz Island looked enormous from the window. That was the rock and sand island where I'd be taken by boat with the other swimmers for the race back to shore. I gazed at the broad expansive beach, miles of blue-green sea, the curving coast, and other red-brown islands—largely devoid of vegetation.

Hungry for dinner, we walked down the beach into the older part of town, settling on a beachfront restaurant called the Totoaba, named after a fish fated to be hunted to near extinction because of a myth that its bladder has magical health properties. A kilo of totoaba bladder is said to sell on the black market for 20 to 80,000 dollars per kilo.

The next morning, I walked to the beach before 6 AM for a warmup swim. The sea was only mid-calf deep even after I waded about 50 meters across the clay-like bottom. I worried stingrays might be lurking in the shallows, as they do in San Carlos. I've never felt the sharp barb of a tail strike my bare foot, but my husband and stepson both had. The jab of a stingray tail is followed by three hours soaking the injured foot in the hottest water tolerable to release the venom and diminish the agony.

Friends who had been stung in San Carlos swore that a shot or two of tequila aided recovery a bit more.

I shuffled my feet until it was deep enough that my hands wouldn't brush the bottom and swam while a glowing full moon slowly descended toward the horizon in the purplish sky. I rolled over and transitioned into a lazy backstroke, gazing up at the moon, smelling the salt and relishing the flow of water all around me and that happy-to-be-alive surge of joy that exercise and feeling at one with nature always brings. I thought about the dolphins in San Carlos and wondered if they would notice my absence as they dove their way up and down the San Francisco Beach shoreline.

After coffee and a light yogurt breakfast, Chris and I walked to the starting line. Swimmers and families were already gathered. Tents, portable bathrooms, and the finish line had been set up. I felt a sudden assault of prerace jitters — on steroids because of it being an international race. The other competitors said they picked up their race stuff in Hermosillo. What about me? Should I have arrived earlier? Was I too late to get my number?

A man directed me to a sign with a list of competitors. I found my number before joining the line of swimmers waiting to have their numbers inked on their shoulders. Then I found the timing chip line.

It soon became clear the race wouldn't start on time. Or, rather, it would start on Mexican time. More and more competitors crowded around, and the line for arm inking had turned serpentine. Several *pangas* or small fishing boats approached the shore and swimmers climbed aboard. I waited until a few boats had gone out, wanting the sun to be higher in the sky before I shed my warm clothes. The water was still chilly — in the mid-70s — and the morning air crisp.

A woman with short, dark hair and a friendly smile ran up to me and asked if I was Susan. Surprised and wondering how she knew my name, I said "yes." Her name was Mimi and she said she'd seen photos of me on Facebook. I thought it was amazing that she recognized me so quickly. She introduced me to her friends from San Diego who had traveled down with her for the race. Mimi had messaged me months earlier, asking about San Carlos. She had grown up in México and now lived in San Diego. It was her dream to return to México, she said.

The easy conversation distracted me from worries over possible seasickness or getting chilled during the boat ride out.

Distractions have served as angels along my spiritual journey. Once when I participated in an online book discussion with a few high school classmates, we were laughing a lot and a migraine disappeared without me even noticing. I had one and then it was gone. It was the first clue that my thoughts were contributing to my illness. When swimming, the migraines would often transform into an itch and then fade away.

Eventually, I made a conscious choice not to focus on fear. Whenever I've been afraid of schedule or food changes on trips or when socializing, I've descended into pain. But on occasions where my faith has been strong enough and I trusted God rather than being afraid — of food or anything else — the next day arrived without painful consequences. My ability — or lack of ability — to manage stress in a particular situation and seeing myself as a spiritual, rather than a vulnerable material being, has more of an impact on my well-being than following all of my better-do-it-or-else rituals to the letter.

We climbed aboard one of the small fishing boats and ten minutes later, we exited at Alcatraz Island. More than 400 swimmers ranging from about age ten up to beyond 80 swam around, waded, and conversed with other swimmers.

A large boat approached. A man speaking over a megaphone instructed us to stay behind the space between his boat and another one across from it until the start. The odor of gasoline fumes was overpowering, and I stifled a cough. Soon the countdown began. Swimmers treading water drifted across the line, seemingly frantic and unable to wait for *uno*.

A loud horn sounded. Arms and legs splashed and thrashed and churned up the water. I had positioned myself to the far right, hopeful I'd avoid major body contact. A hand slapped my arm, another one dragged along my calf. I upped my tempo, furiously pulling my way through the water. Minutes later, I broke free from the crowd. I sighted ahead, looking toward where we'd finish on the beach. But in the brilliant sun, all the white buildings along the shoreline looked the same. I had anticipated being able to see the myriad power lines I'd noticed around the finish. Unfortunately, they weren't visible at water level.

I'd have to follow the lead swimmers and hope they weren't deviating too far off-course. I slowed from a drop-dead sprint into a comfortable rhythm to go the distance. The adrenaline high of the vigorous exercise kicked in, heightening my senses. I savored the embrace of the cool seawater as it slid over my skin, felt the tingle in my face and fingers that was so often part of my swimmer's high.

Many safety personnel had been installed on the course. Some were Hermosillo fire department workers — *bomberos* — installed in boats and kayaks. Some were even in the water swimming with life buoys ready to assist swimmers in sudden trouble.

I swam neck and neck with a lean young boy of 11 or 12. He inspired me to raise my tempo another notch. He'd pull ahead and then I'd push to catch up and stay ahead for a few strokes before he'd be right with me again. By now, I saw the shore clearly. Spectators crowded the wide sandy beach.

With the finish in sight, I kicked harder and increased my turnover. I heard the flow of water and the loud ebb and flow of my labored breathing. About 200 yards from shore, I stood up in the shallows on the hard, clay-like bottom, chasing the young boy just a meter ahead of me. Running through the viscous water seemed easy for him but my legs felt leaden, and the hot, humid air sunk into my lungs. I collapsed back into the shin-deep water, breathless, and swam, relieved to be moving through water again.

I swam on until my hand touched the sand before launching myself upright for a final dash to the finish. I ran through a corridor of cheering spectators across the timing pads, waving and smiling. Lightheaded bliss washed over me. I'd never seen so much enthusiasm at an open water race. A young girl with long hair walked over and congratulated me, placing a finisher's medal around my neck.

Chris and I watched more swimmers sprint or walk from the shallows—transformed to a muddy brown—across the finish line. As the final competitors swam toward shore, including my new friend Mimi, the *bomberos* with buoys accompanied each one of them to the shore. Spectators cheered and clapped, and the sand below my feet vibrated as loud music projected from large speakers. The race—a medley of camaraderie, competition, and conscientious safety, was punctuated by a delightful celebratory and party atmosphere.

Another swimmer in my age group—Katherine—an American woman who now lives in Kino Bay, walked up to congratulate me. I had first met her and her husband at the October open water race in Miramar near San Carlos. Her husband said he had seen the results sheet and that I had placed first in my age group. A thrill of excitement ran through me.

When my name was announced for my age group, I stepped on the top of the podium and held hands with the second and third place finishers and we raised our arms in the air to a thumping bass and cheers from the crowd.

Months later, the race director would tell me I'd set a course record for my age group. This would be the last open water race I would compete in for two years due to the COVID-19 pandemic. In 2022, I raced in Kino Bay again and won my age group for the second time.

CHAPTER THIRTY-TWO

San Carlos, México – March 2020

My mother traveled with us to San Carlos for her first visit ever, planning to a stay a week. COVID-19 cases raged in the U.S. and soon sickened and killed many in México. Our old condo administrator, José, had resigned just weeks earlier. A new administrator—a former CEA water company executive, Roberto, had been hired.

I received a letter from INM, the Mexican immigration office, stating that I had failed to respond to an email about my work status. The timing of having to deal with red tape couldn't have been worse.

There was talk that the U.S.-México border might close. We didn't want my mom trapped south of the border. We didn't want to be separated from our adult children and other family members. It no longer seemed wise for my husband to spend more time in Tucson while I remained in México. We couldn't risk being separated for an indefinite amount of time.

The pandemic was bad in the U.S., but we feared it might be even more devastating in México, a country with far fewer resources to prepare for such a disaster. For all we knew, the country would descend into chaos. We decided to leave as soon as possible, getting my mom safely home to Tucson where we would hunker down for an indeterminate amount of time.

Feeling panicked about needing to leave, I drove to the immigration office to try to rectify the issue with my work documents. I told the female official at the counter that I had never received the email requesting further details about my yoga teaching. She was a young lady—with thick dark hair, smooth skin, a round face and kind eyes. I told her that due to the COVID crisis, we needed to get my elderly mother back to the U.S. as soon as possible and because our whole family lived up there, we likely would not return to México for a long time. She listened to me with a compassionate look in her eyes. I saw fear there, too. And I sensed fear in the the room that swirled like a black cloud around us.

Everything felt scary and uncertain. Did it really matter if she said I couldn't work anymore or that my permanent residency was in jeopardy? I didn't want her to say those things, of course, but as I silently prayed, I told myself that I needed to focus on what mattered most—getting back to Tucson safely.

The woman spoke to a colleague and then returned. She said my work status was in jeopardy but that she would remediate everything immediately so I wouldn't have to worry. She typed up every single document they needed to have on file that I would have otherwise had to prepare a second time myself. The Mexican government loves their paperwork. But Mexican people often demonstrate a level of kindness I've rarely witnessed elsewhere. This patient woman spent at least 90 minutes typing up different documents and having me sign them. I thanked her profusely when we finished and we left the office knowing that if I wanted to return to México to work and live, all was in order.

As I packed my suitcase that night, the reality of our situation hit me. For the first time in three years, I would leave México, the country that now felt like home, uncertain of when I would return. I might not return to my beloved San Carlos for months, or even years.

I lay in bed awake. Maybe we wouldn't survive the pandemic. A deadly, contagious illness was spreading like wildfire. No one really knew what was safe and what wasn't. And there was no vaccine. No cure.

Maybe we'd never come back to México. Maybe I'd never get to swim in the sea again. All the pools in México, the U.S. and many other countries had been closed. That might sound like a minor worry to most people. Losing the water terrified me as much as losing my life. Swimming had been the one anchor hold through all the ups and downs of my life. When we drove away from the Sea of Cortez, my link to the water would be severed.

The morning before we drove north, I took one last swim. A dark dolphin fin knifed through the calm water toward me as I waded into the shallows. The pod of bottlenose dolphins I'd befriended seemed to be waiting for me. Perhaps they sensed that connecting was important that day. Once I swam toward them, many of them glided around me less than a hand's distance away.

Feeling overpowered by emotion, I broke down into sobs. The coronavirus felt like an ominous storm moving in — worse than the tornadoes I'd feared so much as a child. Maybe we wouldn't survive. Maybe this plague would wipe out mankind. I didn't know how to ask God for help in a situation like this.

Maybe this was supposed to happen, maybe it was the only way the earth could be saved.

The dolphins must have sensed my distress. They stayed near me longer than usual, swimming circles around me, displaying their bellies, waving their pectoral fins, blowing bubbles. I told them I had to leave. That something terrible was happening and I didn't know if and when I'd return. I told them I loved them, that they had become my friends, and that because they had come near during my swims, they had brightened so many of my days. I always felt calm near them.

They drifted so close, just inches away. I saw strands of algae trailing behind one dolphin's tail; white scratches etched another's rubbery skin. Red blisters marred another dolphin's face. I wondered if they knew of the peril happening to humankind. Do they ever wonder if our population declined, would the amount of trash diminish? Would the water clear up?

I told them how much I would miss the sea, how I felt like I belonged in the water, how I wanted to stay, how I wished they would carry me away from this nightmare happening on dry land. Two dolphins swam by, looking as though their pectoral fins were linked. Maybe they were showing me how I could hold on. Maybe they were willing to take me away if I wanted. And I did want that. To escape. To not have to face what was to come.

But after a while the dolphins drifted away and I found myself floating alone again in the turquoise Sea of Cortez. I swam toward shore and stood up. I walked across the sand away from the water toward a future without dolphins, without the sea, without swimming.

CHAPTER THIRTY-THREE

Tucson, Arizona – March 2020

Back in Tucson, I tried to reconcile myself to this new life that no one had planned for. Chris and I would get up and drink a cup of coffee while reading the latest horrifying news reports on our iPhones. I knew I should pray and trust God more instead of getting sucked into this mire of terror. Sometimes, I would avoid the news entirely and start off the day meditating and reading my Bible lesson. My best days happened when I read spiritual articles intermittently throughout the day to maintain a sense of calm and balance. On the more difficult days, I'd get distracted by all the bad news and be trembling with anxiety by mid-afternoon. In those moments, it felt like God was inaccessible, the way I feel during a migraine.

We never left the house except to walk or run, or to pick up groceries we'd ordered online at Walmart. People who had taken my yoga class at Bahía Delfín asked if I could teach online and after struggling to figure out the technology, I started teaching a few days a week on Zoom. Never in my life have I received so much thanks for teaching. The participants not only craved the yoga to calm their minds and stretch and strengthen their bodies, they craved the opportunity to connect with others. I felt grateful that I could provide these classes that seemed to help everyone so much.

Isolation became a way of life. My nurse daughter wouldn't visit us because of her constant exposure to COVID at work. My son and his dad formed their own pod and kept to themselves. We did often visit my mom. Her partner, Dick, had moved from her house to assisted living a few months before COVID, and now with lockdowns, she could only see him for window visits. She was so lonely there was no way we would leave her alone. We did our best to minimize our exposure risk. And every day I prayed. That I wouldn't inadvertently cause anyone harm. That we would all survive.

I ran, walked and/or practiced yoga daily, but a part of me felt missing. I was used to exiting the water after my swim, wearing an elated smile on my face, and relishing a calm, sharp state of mind. Yoga calmed me some. But not enough, and the more running miles I put in, the more my body rebelled. The impact exercise didn't agree with my body. It kept saying, please not again. Water, please give me a pool or ocean! I'd done plenty of land exercise before. But never every day like this.

Most nights, I dreamed about swimming. And suddenly the water would drain out of the pool, or I'd run toward the sea and it would keep moving further away or a person would order me to get out of the water and I'd wake up in a cold sweat.

An ER physician and swimmer I knew in Phoenix climbed an aquatic center fence and embarked on a desperate, unauthorized swim. Of course, he ended up getting a stern warning and thrown out of the pool. Another swimmer I knew started swimming in icy rivers and lakes in Colorado. Honestly, I understood why people did crazy things to alleviate water withdrawal. I certainly thought about it. Fantasized about it, actually.

After two weeks, I begged my ex-husband to let me swim laps in his backyard pool. He kindly agreed. The water was about 60 degrees, but at this point, I didn't care. It became part of my almost daily routine. The drive to Sterling's pool was one of the few ventures away from the house, other than to visit my mom or pick up groceries. It became the highlight of my day. Sure, it was only nine strokes to the other end, and hypothermia struck by the time I exited, but I was moving through water. I felt a ridiculous amount of gratitude to be able to do this. I thanked Sterling profusely every time and sometimes took small gifts to show my appreciation. Honestly, the difference it made in my mental health was huge.

Chris and I morphed into recluses. We were both introverted in the first place but now we could barely start a conversation with someone we saw on the trail. I read books on my Kindle and wrote a series of online yoga articles for U.S. Masters Swimming. I dumped many thoughts into a journal. My crazy, tangled up thoughts.

I'd listen to Doja Cat songs in the car and think, whenever I hear this song years from now, I'm going to remember this dreadful pandemic. I wondered if other people I passed driving their cars were thinking similar thoughts. Will I still be alive next year? Will everyone in my family? Please, God, help us.

Every day seemed like a repeat of the same horrible nightmare. One that we kept waking up to again and again—like Bill Murray experienced in the 90s movie *Groundhog Day*. We even ended up watching the movie once so we could laugh about it.

Material life isn't supposed to be real. The Toltecs believed that. Jesus demonstrated that. Mary Baker Eddy taught that. I had been studying Christian Science and attending online church services and had experienced recent healings from a back injury and a urinary tract infection. But the pandemic had enshrouded me with an isolation like I never imagined. I felt cut off from my family and friends. Worst of all, I felt like I was slipping out of God's comforting embrace.

CHAPTER THIRTY-FOUR

San Carlos, México – May 2020

"What is life? A madness.
What is life? An illusion, a shadow, a story.
And the greatest good is little enough; for all life is a dream,
and dreams themselves are only dreams."
Pedro Calderón de la Barca – Spanish poet

I followed Facebook posts and emails from friends and others who had remained in México. Most U.S. states were still on lockdown. People were prohibited from taking car trips and traveling—not that this government mandate stopped anyone. I'd drive to Sterling's house to swim and spot license plates from Michigan, Iowa, Montana, Maryland, and New Jersey.

When I returned home, I'd browse Facebook and learn that drivers were crossing the border into México without issues if it was considered "essential travel." And Americans were returning to the States from south of the border, *no problema.*

Since we owned homes in both countries, we had a reason to travel — to take care of one home or the other.

I grew restless. Every fiber of my being ached to swim — really swim — more than nine strokes at a time. I missed the beach. I missed the dolphins. I longed to tell Nick and the others in the pod we were still alive. Please, please, can we go, I asked Chris.

Within days, we were packed and driving toward Nogales. We had more masks with us than water bottles. Anxiety raced through my veins. I'd heard rumors about Mexicans protesting at the border, panicked that visiting Americans would spread illness. An article in a Tucson paper included a photo of a "sanitation tunnel" at the border where Americans were being ordered to walk through. I didn't want to enter if I was going to be sprayed by noxious chemicals.

The pandemic had stolen my adventurous nature. Staying at home felt like the norm after almost two months of going close to nowhere. I fidgeted and gnawed at my fingernails whenever both hands weren't on the wheel. Disaster scenarios ran through my mind. I tried to ward off these dark fears with prayers, but it was difficult. Outside the house, I felt vulnerable. Uneasy. But we had to move forward. It was the only way to break free from the isolation and the too-long withdrawal from real swimming.

The Third Sutra in Book One of Patanjali's Yoga Sutras translates as "Then the Seer (Self) abides in its own nature." He means that if your mind is calm, you not only see life more clearly, but you can express and experience your authentic self. To accomplish that, you must restrain the modifications of the mind, which he writes about in the first sutra. Basically, in your mind, you cultivate an experience of suffering or an experience of contentment. The outside world doesn't have to disturb your state of mind anymore. Your mind can be steady, quiet, and harmonious regardless of what happens around you.

Life in 2020 was a scary place—filled with restrictions, fear, and alarming statistics. I started and ended every day with prayer and spiritual study. But I wasn't keeping my mind steady. Mind chatter and fear kept intruding.

Emotions tend to be contagious—and can be "caught" by others for better or worse. People tend to radiate either positive or negative energy or their energy can shift from day to day, from hour to hour. I've experienced energy shifts in many of my fitness and yoga classes. An upbeat crowd can lift the whole atmosphere while one angry, negative person can detract from the positive experience I want to give my participants.

What we allow into our thoughts matters. It affects our day and experience. What we're thinking also can bleed into the consciousnesses of people around us, particularly if they are sensitive. Most people tend to see what was wrong with everyone around them.

One reason Jesus could heal ailing people is that he recognized them as God's creations—as spiritual and perfect—instead of believing their limited, material condition was their reality. Everyone else tended to see a leper or a mentally unstable person or whatever quality was less-than-good in someone. In every instance, Jesus saw past those illusions, which brought about transformation.

I heard reports that people were packing on extra pounds, getting out of shape, falling into the darkness of depression, and buying record amounts of alcohol. It was the only way people knew how to cope with the isolation and terror. I couldn't imagine succumbing to that—constantly numbing my mind to get through another day.

My parents never drank alcohol. Christian Scientists normally don't. They don't use drugs, either. They live a spiritually-based life.

Most people mistakenly think Christian Science is a cult. It isn't—it's a Christian religion. We study the Bible and a book (first published in 1875) by the church's founder, Mary Baker Eddy, called *Science and Health with Key to the Scriptures*. A common misconception is that Christian Scientists don't go to doctors. The truth is more nuanced; some do, and some don't. We believe that Jesus healed people from various illnesses and disabilities because he understood the power and presence of God's love. We also believe that this healing power is available to everyone.

Many Christian Scientists use prayer to heal illnesses and cope with day-to-day problems, but almost everyone gets dental work, many get joint surgeries, and some seek a doctor's care under certain circumstances. It's all about a continuum of trust. Some people trust God more and require no medical intervention. Others have trust in certain situations and may seek a physician's help if it seems like the right thing to do.

In *Science and Health*, founder Mary Baker Eddy encouraged her followers to "emerge gently from matter into Spirit." Following practical steps to enhance one's physical and mental health aren't considered contradictory to our beliefs. Many of us exercise and pursue healthy eating and sleeping habits.

Many people—whether Christian Scientists or not—experience improved health once they uncover the root cause of their illnesses and remediate these rather than swallowing another pill to fix the body after it's broken so to speak. I find that when I take good care of myself, I think less about my body and can focus more on growing spiritually and helping others.

A fundamental premise of Christian Science is that matter does not define us. God created us in a spiritual, non-flawed form. Material existence is more dream than reality. If we awaken to our connection to God and our spiritual being, we can essentially transcend the limits of a material body.

Does this sound crazy? Some people say so. But many Christian Scientists living into their 80s, 90s, and beyond take no medications, have been healed of illnesses — including COVID — and experience excellent health. My mom is only one example. My grandmother Ballantyne — a Christian Science practitioner or healer — took calls from people in need until she was in her 90s and lived to be 104.

Miracles can happen to anyone whenever the mind is quiet and open to God's angel messages. On three occasions, events happened to me that demonstrated God was looking out for me.

Several months had passed since I'd started dating Sterling, my now ex-husband. One night, I heard a deep, disturbing voice in a dream, say, "You're pregnant." At that stage in my life, I often bragged to friends that I was never going to have kids. I relished my freedom and couldn't imagine myself tied down. The words from my dream sent me into a panic. I shouted and screamed, "No, no, no!" I didn't want to be pregnant.

All at once, I heard a different voice, very calm and soothing say, "It's going to be all right." The voice seemed to embrace my entire being and I felt a light, buoyant sense of joy and calm like I've never experienced before. It just moved like a wave through my mind and my body. And I felt overwhelmingly happy and grateful that I would become a mother.

When I awakened, I knew right away I was pregnant. Not only that, the pervasive calm, joy and peace that I'd experienced while being verbally and physically embraced by a Divine presence continued to prevail. The logistics didn't concern me. Whatever I needed to do to take care of this child, I would do it. Two days later, at the student health center, a test confirmed pregnancy. In March of the following year, my daughter Marion was born.

Even before that, my father saved my life by listening to and acting on an angel message when I was a junior at Clemson. A one-night stand had left me feeling guilty. I had been drinking a lot and felt lost. One of my best friends had been out of town that week. I felt so alone and empty and needed badly to talk to someone. Unable to overcome the misery of my self-loathing, I considered suicide.

My dad called me out of the blue and said he planned to drive down from Ohio to visit that weekend. Tears streamed down my face when I spoke to him. I told him I looked forward to seeing him. He somehow knew I was in peril. I knew God had given him a message that I needed help. He came to visit and a weekend that could have ended in tragedy turned out to be a beautiful time of connection.

My father saved me a second time when he gifted me a book by Edward A. Kimball accompanied by a letter encouraging me to return to Christian Science. I didn't know then that he was already sick with cancer, but he must have known. He probably thought it might be his last opportunity to help me find a better way of living.

I'd reread the letter from time to time. But I resisted my father's suggestion for another decade after his death. My mom pleaded with me to call a Christian Science Practitioner when my migraines worsened. I told her no. She called one anyway three years ago.

After a few days, I realized fear and sheer obstinance were keeping me from opening my mind to what some refer to as faith healing, but can be more accurately described as transformed existence due to spiritual understanding. I communicated with the practitioner — based in Albuquerque — and established a comfortable connection with him and another practitioner from Switzerland that I met on Facebook. The practitioner in New Mexico was a regular contributor to the Christian Science periodicals — and wrote about overcoming challenges while hiking, long distance running, and scuba diving. I bookmarked many of his articles in an online account and reread them whenever I need inspiration.

Now, I'm living a spiritual lifestyle. I meditate daily and practice yoga often. I read and study the Bible, the *Science and Health*, and other Christian Science literature. I even occasionally publish articles and podcasts to help other spiritual seekers.

Just like I become a stronger swimmer by putting in miles in the water, I become a stronger and more confident disciple by turning to God instead of panicking when facing an illness, a personal conflict, or a difficult to solve problem.

I do believe there is much more to life than the physical body and our physical existence. In the Bible, Jesus repeatedly demonstrated his ability to overcome the laws of physics — feeding large groups of people with little food, transforming water into wine, healing people of almost every kind of illness, stilling storms — and ultimately, returning to life and breath after men did everything in their power to destroy him and his healing ministry. A person doesn't have to be a Christian Scientist to experience healing — it can happen to anyone who lives a spiritual lifestyle and understands God's power.

Now let me share one more story — the path that led me to Chris. We had met at the Barnes and Noble bookstore through a dating network. Our first encounter led only to occasional chats on the phone. Weeks later, I was sitting at my computer at home, listening to rain beat on the windows, when a thought came that I should go back to that bookstore. At first, I resisted because it was easier to stay inside than go out in a rainstorm. But then it became clear that there was a reason I was supposed to go. And I listened.

After driving to Barnes and Noble, I found a book and sat down in a plush chair to read. I looked up a bit later to see Chris sitting across from me. I walked over and started up a conversation and he invited me to go with him to a nearby restaurant for dinner. We shared stories about our children, our work, and our years growing up. The bond we formed that evening served as a springboard for a wonderful friendship and romance that led to a longlasting marriage.

Perseverance and commitment are required to set a marriage on a firm foundation. Those same qualities can help a person cope with feeling less than 100 percent. I've noticed how some people barely notice discomfort while others complain about it often. On drives, like we were taking to México that day, we often face urgent needs to use the restroom, hunger, and long waits at the border, immigration, and/or toll booths.

We can ask God's help when coping with pain and discomfort. We can declare our unity with God and that only he—not pain or illness—has dominion over our lives. On page 393 of *Science and Health*, Mary Baker Eddy encourages followers to "Take possession of your body and govern its feeling and action." In II Corinthians (King James version, 5:8), it says, "We are confident, I say, and willing to be absent from the body, and to be present with the Lord." Focusing more on what God calls us to do makes it possible to break free from cumbersome material limitations.

The yoga path isn't dissimilar to the Christian Science spiritual path. Regular meditation and yoga practice has enabled yogis and mystics to transcend physical and mental limitations, achieving states of bliss and divine connection known as *samadhi*. In this elevated state of being, you can experience your divine consciousness, feel a sense of unity with the Divine, and are not limited by material laws.

Yogis typically study the sutras—a set of scriptures on yogic theory written by the sage Patanjali around 500 B.C. that outline the eight limbs of yoga. According to these precepts, you aim to live an ethical, non-harming, compassionate life and engage in yoga and meditation to cleanse your mind of clutter, day by day improving concentration and focus until you are readily able to connect with your true self and your concept of the Divine.

The eight limbs of yoga include the fifth limb or *pratyahara*, which is Sanskrit for withdrawal of the senses. The whole purpose of this exercise, accomplished through yoga practice and breathing (*pranayama*), is to become disciplined enough that you can smell fresh chocolate chip cookies or hear the phone ring without giving into the temptation to stop your current task—whether it is a work project or your meditation practice.

In *Light on the Yoga Sutras of Patanjali*, the now deceased yoga guru B.K.S. Iyengar wrote, "In *samadhi*, awareness of place vanishes, and one ceases to experience space and time."

The Toltecs and many poets and philosophers believed life to be a dream. What I believe is that everything we experience with our five physical senses is more illusion than truth. There are many spiritual paths to truth, and it is up to each person to find the path that leads to his or her own enlightenment. No journey is a straight line. The journey I'm on is rife with hills and valleys.

We approached the Hermosillo bypass tollbooth. I saw what I thought was a police car parked beyond it. I pointed it out to Chris. After handing my money to the attendant, the gate opened and I slowly drove ahead, holding my breath. Chris and I both expected a person to step from the car and stop us.

What if the officer said we had to turn around and return to Tucson? As we drove closer, we both burst into laughter. What had appeared to be a police car was only a large cardboard form that had been installed next to the road — probably to get people to slow down. Things indeed are not always what they seem to be.

90 minutes later, we exited Mex-15. Blocky white letters on a rocky desert hill I'd dubbed Star Wars Mountain spelled out San Carlos. We encountered a roadblock on our way into town. I confidently removed a recent utility bill with our names and addresses from the truck console. I told the soldier from the National Guard we were going to our residence at Bahía Delfín. He permitted us to pass. A few minutes later, our journey ended.

I ran barefoot down to the sea and shouted with joy. All I could hear was the wind and the crash of waves on the sand. I ran into the water up to my waist, relishing the embrace of the sea. I could swim whenever I wanted again. I was home.

CHAPTER THIRTY-FIVE

San Carlos, México – July 2020

The only illness spreading faster than COVID was selfishness. Many Americans thought their rights to "have fun" and "get back to normal" mattered more than following simple protocols and measures that protected the health of their fellow Americans. How difficult was it to wear a mask, really? I mean, sure, it was annoying, but most of us only had to wear one for 30 minutes in a store or a couple of hours on a flight.

While 9/11 had brought everyone together, COVID seemed to be pulling everyone apart. What had gone wrong? Why couldn't people suppress their own petty wants long enough to consider the difficulties endured by healthcare workers? It made me angry that people claimed that COVID was a hoax when my nurse daughter bore witness to the intubation and death of patients almost daily at the hospital.

Some people might imagine my Christian Science beliefs would lead me to shun mask wearing. Yet that's far from the truth. Mary Baker Eddy encouraged her followers to cooperate with public officials concerning health crises. I wanted to act in a kind and ethical way. I followed the *ahimsa* (non-harming) principal of yoga (part of the first limb). And I followed the second commandment (Mark 12:31, King James version of the Bible), which reads, "Thou shalt love thy neighbor as thyself." To me, that means that I should be kind to people and not do anything that would cause them fear or harm (including illness). I wore a mask whenever I was in public and eventually got vaccinated without complaint.

Despite the N95 masks Marion wore to work that gave her headaches, she still managed to contract the disease. She stayed home, ill and in isolation while family and friends brought her groceries, medications, and anything we could think of to cheer her up. But we couldn't spend time with her. Those 14 days of isolation time were lonely and traumatic for her.

Meanwhile, the Mexican government closed the beaches to reduce the spread of COVID. Mexican officials had dug big trenches across the dirt roads leading to the beach to discourage people from beach outings. Fortunately, outdoor exercise by then had been permitted.

The sea was the one place I felt free from pandemic worries. One morning, when tropical storm Christina was spinning westward in the Pacific off Baja, Chris and I went to the beach and encountered rough seas. Looking for calmer water, we walked toward the estuary. "Oh, look, the dolphins." I pointed them out to Chris.

I watched them and felt that familiar rush of excitement. I couldn't wait to get in the water. "I'm going to swim out," I said.

Chris thought it was too rough. "I'll swim toward the estuary, and you can walk that way and join me where it's calmer," I told him.

He warned me to be careful before I waded in and battled to swim past the surf. The water looked midnight blue — almost black. I swam parallel to shore toward the estuary. It was easy to clock my husband in his bright orange swim trunks strolling along on the sand. Chris was walking slowly, matching my swimming speed, probably concerned about me being out alone with the waves.

I wished he wouldn't worry about me. By now, I'd done so much sea swimming, being out in open water under various conditions felt routine. Tremors of anxiety were rare. Most often, I felt an amazing sense of peace. I often felt God's presence. Being surrounded by water felt like a divine embrace comforting and reassuring me.

A towering wave raised me up high and then dropped me down into a trough. Again and again, I experienced that rhythmic rise and fall. I pushed aside visions of a rogue wave crashing over me then tumbling me around like a fast spin cycle. A few times while out boogie boarding in southern California, I'd been churned around and bashed into the sand by waves.

I can handle some swells, I told myself, as I continued bilateral breathing, rolling my head until my mouth almost faced the sky to avoid inhaling water.

Eventually, the sea quieted and Chris swam out to join me. The pod of dolphins drifted in our direction. Layers of puffy clouds obscured the sun, but the water was clear and every dolphin body that glided by stood out in sharp detail. I saw the elongated white masks around their eyes, their white bellies, and the long lines of blunt white teeth whenever they opened their mouths. The dolphins seemed to enjoy showing off. *Look at my belly. Look at my teeth. Hey, I've got a name for you. But I bet you don't understand it since you aren't good with dolphin speak.*

I hadn't seen Nick since the pandemic began. I've often wondered if something happened to him or if he had split from the pod. Maybe his dorsal fin healed, making it impossible for me to distinguish him from the other males?

Another morning a dolphin swam toward me and gazed at me face to face. She spoke to me in screechy dolphin chatter and then presented me with a piece of litter—a Cheetos bag. This was the second time a dolphin had brought me trash, "requesting" that I remove it from their environment. On an earlier occasion, a large dark body had glided underneath me with a light-colored object on its dorsal fin. One flick of the tail and the big white plastic bag popped up underneath me. Maybe they see me picking up trash on the beach and know I will gladly remove it. Trying to see life from a dolphin's point of view is a regular exercise for me.

Rarely, the dolphins are quiet. More often, their sounds give them away and I hear them before I see them. Today, they were super vocal. Chatter echoed through the water. Whistles and clicking noises were constant. *Here, check out this human with the weird orange floaty thing*, a mother may have said in dolphin speak to the two-foot-long baby swimming almost on top of her back.

I spotted another larger juvenile dolphin. Others glided near and then swam away. I watched the turned-out tips of their flukes disappear into the depths. Sometimes six or seven pod members swam underneath us all at once. Dolphins navigate with so much precision and control. A tail that looked like it would strike me in the face would float past inches beneath me.

One dolphin glided up to face me nose to nose. This happened often. He paused to study me. What was he so curious about? Did he wonder about the strange goggles I wore over my eyes and why some humans but not all wore them when swimming?

Dolphins appear to wear a perpetual smile on their faces, which makes me wonder if they're always happy or just look that way. The corners of my mouth turn down (despite my attempts at trying face yoga to rectify this) and people sometimes think I'm not happy when most of the time, I am content. Looks can be deceiving.

While our thoughts revolve around work issues, paying the bills, health concerns, and spending time with our loved ones, dolphins must think about catching food, avoiding predators, health issues, and communicating with and enjoying the companionship of their pod. I wonder if they experience stress the way we do or if they discuss ways to relax and find better balance in their lives. I wonder if they pray.

I know for sure that dolphins like to play. That's what humans tend to forget to do after childhood. The fun element is lost, and life starts to become a long series of obligations. My dolphin friends remind me to bring play back into my life. It is a wonderful escape from worries, a welcome release to experience a few moments of childlike joy and elation. Dancing around the room to a favorite song, laughing out loud with a friend, turning a cartwheel, or throwing a frisbee on the beach are also ways I like to bring back that youthful elation. Along with swimming with dolphins, of course!

A few dolphins began to body surf. Conditions were right for it—and they savored the opportunity. I watched them soar over the waves, moving rapidly toward shore. Their bodies are so streamlined and buoyant, ideal for wave surfing. They came over to visit with us repeatedly. And then they glided underneath us, apparently taking a very deep breath, because all at once they were gone. And Chris and I were alone out in the waves.

Have a good day, I said underwater, even though I knew they were probably hundreds of feet away by then. Every time I swim with the pod, it feels like such a privilege. I feel so blessed that for this sliver of time, they choose to offer me a close-up view of their unique world.

CHAPTER THIRTY-SIX

San Carlos, México – July 2020

A family renting condo 167 set up their canopy near ours. Mom, dad, and two eight-year-old twin boys all wore their cloth masks whenever at the beach. The parents spent hours outside playing with them, despite the oppressive heat. They stayed at Bahía Delfín for two weeks while tile work was being done in their Sahuarita, Arizona home.

I was reading under my beach tent one morning when I heard the two boys fighting. One was whacking a piece of wood with a stick. The other was yelling at him to stop.

Sometimes I want to reach out to people when conflict happens. I sometimes don't follow through — because of lack of confidence. I'm always worried my attempt to help will fail or that I'll feel awkward. I know in some ways this reluctance is a kind of selfishness. I should be focused on the person who needs help instead of my unease.

I asked the two boys why they were fighting. I felt at ease and that God was helping me to say the right words. One brother said the other had taken his stick and wouldn't give it back. Instead of getting drawn into the debate, I asked the boys if they liked outdoor games. Wide eyed with enthusiasm, they said, "yes" at the same time.

When I brought out the squishy balls and paddle ball set that had sat unused on a shelf in my closet for months, they snatched them from my hands with excitement.

The rest of the day, the brothers played harmoniously together without conflict. I felt grateful that God had led me to intervene. Everything had worked out favorably and I knew that would give me the courage to act the next time something happened.

The night before their return to Arizona, the twins returned the toys they had borrowed. The boy named Aiden gave me a refrigerator magnet cat that his mom explained was Crookshanks, Hermione Granger's cat from the Harry Potter books. I thanked Aiden and told them they could play with the toys again the next time they visited San Carlos.

Later in the summer, I had another opportunity to help someone. I was under my tent dozing when I heard someone sobbing. I had a horrible headache and worried I wouldn't be alert enough to help. I swung my head around to see a young girl—perhaps nine years old—sitting hunched over on the sea wall, head bowed, her body trembling as she sobbed in total despair. I temporarily forgot my suffering as I strode toward her, unsure whether to speak to her in English or Spanish. I asked in Spanish what her name was.

She looked up at me and started mumbling in hysterical English. Her name was Natalie. She had gotten separated from her family while playing on the beach. She couldn't find them. They were staying in a white building, she said. I looked at her wrist band and saw she was staying at Pilar. I said with confidence that her parents were nearby and that I knew where they were staying.

Let's walk there now, I suggested. She instantly transformed from despair to joyful excitement—running and skipping ahead of me, her braided pigtails flopping against her back, her distress forgotten. Fortunately, I didn't even have to take her to the office. Her family stood on the grass just inside the property boundary. I felt grateful I had been able to lead Natalie home.

CHAPTER THIRTY-SEVEN

San Carlos, México - July 12, 2020

"When one is a stranger to oneself then one is estranged from others too. If one is out of touch with oneself, then one cannot touch others."
Gift from the Sea – Anne Morrow Lindbergh

We'd been in San Carlos for nearly two months and were only days away from returning to Tucson. I felt weighed down by sadness. I didn't want to go back to the intense summer heat and pandemic chaos. People in the States were punching each other in grocery stores and raging at each other over masks. I didn't want to deal with it. I wanted to stay on my isolated beach where I could pretend all this anger, disconnection, and suffering weren't happening.

When we shopped in México, everyone complied with regulations. Having a monitor at the door ensured that. You entered the store wearing your mask—only one person per family—put your forehead up to the digital thermometer and if the reading was normal, the COVID police person would wave you on and ask you to walk across the disinfected pad and apply sanitizer to your hands.

On days we didn't shop, the pandemic barely crossed my mind. I'd wake up, do a 15-minute meditation, read the Bible lesson, and take a rejuvenating swim. Chris did most of that with me, sometimes substituting a run or a TRX workout for the swim. After breakfast, I'd spend hours under the beach tent, feeling the sea breeze on my skin and watching the brilliant blue water, hearing the soft lull of the waves and the call of passing seabirds.

I was dozing under our beach canopy when a cheeping bird woke me. I opened my eyes, expecting to see a hopeful sparrow craving popcorn or chips. Instead, I saw a tiny bird dart out from under my chair. He was completely adorable. A tiny white and brown bird with a little fluffy crown of feathers on his head. He chirruped frantically. When I carefully stood up from my chair he ran over and stood on one of my feet. Tears filled my eyes, I felt so sorry for him, struggling to survive in this sweltering heat. Temperatures were rising into the high 90s. And this vulnerable little guy was obviously separated from his family.

I messaged Elsa from CRRIFS to see if she could help him. She and Eduardo would come as soon as they could, she said. The tiny bird ran this way and that, confused and frustrated. Eventually, he ran over to the sea wall. Then he came back again. A second time, when I glanced at my phone to see if Elsa had messaged me, he disappeared again. I prayed that I would find him. I walked around and heard his song in the hedges along the west side of the Bahía Delfín property. I wondered if there was a nest in there or if he was alone.

Hours later, after I had returned to our condo, I spotted Elsa and Eduardo from our sliding door window. I went outside to talk with them. They had been looking for the bird to no avail. Instead of the high-pitched cheeping sound, I heard only silence. Had the poor guy perished in the terrible heat?

Maybe he recognized my voice because suddenly the little bird dashed out of the bushes, and Eduardo gently picked him up with a gloved hand. He and Elsa needed a box, so I went back to the condo to get one. After adding a layer of sand, they gently placed the small bird inside. They told me he was a baby Gambel's quail.

They walked around the nearby desert area to look for the little guy's family. They were unable to find one with birds that young. They tried introducing him to a family with larger juveniles, but they wouldn't accept him. In the end, Elsa took him home.

I got a report a day later that he was eating tortillas and drinking water. Soon, he advanced to eating chicken feed. Sometimes, Elsa said, the little guy would curl up in her hand and fall asleep. It warmed my heart to hear this, and every morning I prayed that he would stay alive and be able to be released to the wild one day.

After we returned to Tucson, I prayed for the little guy for a day or two and then became distracted by other things. The little quail drifted further and further from my mind. Eventually, I forgot to keep praying for him.

I later learned from Elsa that he had gotten weaker, stopped eating, and eventually died. When I heard this, my body sagged with sorrow. I believe that spiritual life never ends but I still had hoped the baby quail would be granted a full life on earth. I wondered if I'd kept him in my prayers if he might have lived.

I believe that prayer ushers in the divine power, and that anything can happen. It isn't the length of the prayer, it's the level of faith and the ability to see beyond the material picture to what is actually there — spiritual perfection. And animals and humans can respond to that.

CHAPTER THIRTY-EIGHT

San Carlos, México – September 2020

I sat reading on the couch inside our home-away-from-home condo in San Carlos, México. I felt relieved to be sheltered from the wind and scorching sun after hours of outdoor turtle volunteer activities. Our CRRIFS sea turtle volunteer season was in full swing, with me or other beach patrollers finding new nests almost daily.

A gusty wind frosted the blue-green sea with white caps and swept around our building with a haunting howl. Rising sand and dust hazed the usually clear view from my window of the Sea of Cortez and its rocky volcanic coastline.

I set down my book when I heard a knock. A sea turtle had come up on the beach in broad daylight nearby, my neighbor Buki said. He knew I was a sea turtle rescue volunteer. 2020 marked my second year volunteering with the group, which includes a core group of scientists, as well as local volunteers, and seasonal residents from Canada and the United States.

A turtle on the beach could mean only one thing—a mother turtle in search of a nesting spot. Most often sea turtles nest in the middle of the night. This daylight occurrence would offer me a rare opportunity to witness a miracle. My neighbor described the location and I said I'd notify the rescue group and head out.

Most of the sea turtles in the San Carlos area are Olive Ridleys, which typically nest in the area from June through November. Olive Ridleys are smaller than the other six species of sea turtles found in México. They have olive-colored carapaces, and one or two visible claws on each of their four flippers.

Blowing sand pelted my skin while I strode down the beach. Putting one foot in front of the other was difficult. I felt physically exhausted. I'd already patrolled a section of beach and driven to the incubation room to record temperature readings and check the nests.

The wind snatched my hat from my head, and I had to run down the beach to catch it. I tightened the strap and held onto it as I approached the El Soldado Estuary.

I studied the sand for tracks or visible trails where the turtle's shell and flippers had dragged through the sand. However, the high tide—beginning to recede—had obscured the tracks in the wet sand while the wind had blown away all evidence of the tracks in the dry sand. I queried three swimsuit-clad Mexican teenagers stretched out on towels. "Did you see a sea turtle?" I asked in Spanish.

The young man and two girls wearing bikinis introduced themselves with excited voices and bright eyes. They had initially thought the sea turtle was a discarded tire and had been surprised to see the blackish-green object move.

They walked me up to the top of a dune, mostly obscured by succulent plants. The turtle was digging a hole with her flippers. She had already excavated four other spots, apparently finding them unsuitable for her babies.

We watched from about 15 feet away as we'd been instructed to do during our training. Fast movements or a too-close intrusion can cause a mother turtle to abort the nesting process and flee back to the water.

I was gratified these high school kids so excitedly witnessed this event. I said it was unusual to see nesting during the day, since most sea turtles nest at night.

Tears welled up in Veronica's eyes as she watched the mother turtle. She and her friends Marisol and Hector requested our organization's phone number, eager to join the volunteer team. These youth might brighten the uncertain future for Sonora beaches and the area wildlife. People in México and other coastal countries need to be taught to care about sea turtles enough to fight for them since humans pose a major threat.

Most Mexican states—including Sonora—lag behind in taking key steps necessary to protect endangered wildlife. Lights from developments—mistaken for the moon or the sun—may mislead mothers and new hatchlings away from the sea.

Beach roaming ATVs and vehicles compact the sand when they drive over nests, making it impossible for the hatchlings to emerge. Baby sea turtles that do emerge often fall into tire tracks and perish before they can reach the water.

Fishermen lurking out on the sea at night sometimes steal sea turtle eggs from their nests or capture and kill nesting mothers, despite protection laws against poaching. Sea turtle eggs and turtle products fetch a hefty price on the black market.

The mother turtle waddled down the slope of the dune and started digging a sixth hole. Using her flippers as shovels, she dug downward. The other five spots hadn't been right. She continued scattering sand before pausing and tipping her body upward. She'd finally found her preferred egg-laying spot.

Two other turtle rescue volunteers arrived. The nests can't be left in place because of vehicle and ATV activities on our beaches. We would evacuate the ping-pong ball sized eggs once the mother turtle returned to the sea. The eggs would be housed in our incubation facility, where they could mature in safety.

We watched in awe as the mother turtle sat immobile, depositing what could be hundreds of eggs, before carefully covering the nest—rocking side to side and flinging sand. A few times she stopped and gasped, beak open wide, breathless. This sea creature had left her natural sea habitat, struggling on dry land for nearly two hours to accomplish her mission.

Her labor complete, the mother turtle propelled herself toward the sea at a rapid tempo. She would never see her babies again. A wave washed over her and soon her dark carapace vanished beneath the turbulent waves. We expressed our awe and gratitude at having witnessed this miracle of nature.

My fatigue had melted away. The experience reminded me how fortunate I am to be a turtle rescue volunteer. Man's presence on Earth makes it difficult for baby turtles to survive. The group's efforts give these endangered sea turtles a chance to beat the odds and live.

CHAPTER THIRTY-NINE

San Carlos, México – October 2020

It had been a year and a half since we'd had to put our 14-year-old Chow Chow, Sugar, to sleep. Her suffering had been traumatic to witness. The pain of losing her had begun to fade, but I still felt an *I don't know if I can go through that again* ache whenever I thought of adopting a new dog. I knew Chris felt this way, too, because we often talked about it.

It seemed we might remain dogless indefinitely until Chris joined a Chow Chow group on Facebook. He shared a few pics and soon I joined. First, it was the Chow Chows of Canada and then it was the Our Chow Village and the Chow Chow Rescue Society. We'd tag each other when we saw an especially cute Chow and ooh and aah over how soft and adorable they looked.

When Sugar had still been alive, I'd noticed that the dolphins liked to look at her. Whenever I'd walk her, one or two pod members would swim close to shore. When they

245

wanted to get an especially good look, they would leap from the water. They can get the best view of objects on land that way.

I often wondered if they had noticed when we returned to México from Arizona last April without our dog. Did they wonder what had happened to Sugar? Or did they know? They must have seen other dog owners and watched them walk on the beach together with their pets so many times like best buddies up until the day the dog suddenly went missing. Did they know that by some unfair decree dogs had a shorter lifespan than humans? Did they notice more of a slouch in posture, a sadness in my walk? Did they know bereaved owners strolled on alone not by choice, but because their friends had left this earth?

A post about a Chow in desperate need of an owner grabbed my attention. The dog had been found nearly drowned in a water canal in Yuma, near Arizona's border with California. Before I considered the consequences, I contacted the poster to ask about the dog. But the logistics were complicated, and Chris and I didn't feel ready to take drastic steps to adopt a dog. We weren't even sure we were ready under even the best of circumstances.

The woman suggested that we join the Houston Chow Chow Connection Facebook page. She said they had lots of Chows and had volunteer pilots that could transport the dogs so we wouldn't have to drive a long distance overnight to pick one up—which wasn't exactly convenient in the middle of a pandemic. Often adoptions must happen ASAP because workers at many shelters don't understand the Chow Chow temperament, deem them dangerous, and put them to sleep.

Chris and I browsed the site, checking out all the dog photos. In the beginning, it was just for fun. We'd look at pictures and see which dogs needed homes. But in the back of our minds, we remembered how hard it had always been to get Sugar to eat, how often she'd been sick. But before long, our worries about inconvenience waned and our curiosity about these adorable Chows transformed to longing. We wanted to adopt one.

We called to ask about some of the dogs. There were two Chow Chows that caught our attention — Tenny and Chief. The short-legged, fluffy brown Tenny was in Houston and fluffy white Chief was in Iowa. Either could be transported by plane to Tucson.

Now we had to determine which dog — if either — was right for us. In the past, we'd always gone to shelters and spent hours hanging out with a dog before bringing him or her home. In this instance, we had to settle for Facetime video sessions, which was less than ideal.

Three-year-old Chief had a complicated history. He'd been in countless foster situations. It looked like he'd found a lifelong home after an older woman in Iowa adopted him. Life was good until her eight-year-old grandson came over to her house one day and rammed Chief in the head with his toy car while blasting a horn in his ear. Chief bit the boy in the face and he required several stitches. The child's mother was so angry she said in no uncertain terms that the dog would have to go, or grandma would never see her grandson again. So, poor Chief was out the door and taken to a person caring for dozens of dogs, living outdoors in a cage.

We were notified that Tenny — the other dog we were considering — had another family interested in adopting him. No one wanted Chief. I felt so sorry for him. He'd had such bad luck. I kept thinking if the grandmother had been more careful and kept her grandson from misbehaving, maybe the biting incident wouldn't have happened. The video sessions showed him to be a little sad, bored, and easily startled. But he didn't seem aggressive or mean.

I feared that Chief's past would keep him from finding a home. And I wanted to give him a chance. Our children were grown and if our granddaughter Isabelle came to visit, we would be able to watch closely to make sure she didn't tease him.

Chris and I were both scared to commit. Taking care of a dog is a big responsibility. But the more we talked about it, the more we believed we were the answers to Chief's prayers. At the end of the week, we signed the adoption papers.

A month later, he was flown from Iowa to New Mexico, then on to Tucson. Chris met him at the airport and a few days later, drove him down to San Carlos. We loved our big white fluffy boy Chief right away. He has big dark eyes accented by angled dents-in-his-fur brows, pointy ears and like all Chows, a black tongue and a turned-up tail (it only droops down if he's not happy).

Chief instantly took to the beach life. He loves digging in the grass, digging in the sand, peeing on every sandcastle and other mound of sand, and sniffing out seaweed. We have to pull him away from dead birds and fish that wash up—that to him smell delicious, apparently. Our fluffy Chow Chow doesn't swim much, but he makes a beeline toward the water and wades up to his chin whenever he gets too hot.

At first, Chief must have thought his new living situation was too good to be true. He must have worried that as fast as he'd been out of his last home, he'd be tossed out of ours. He scratched himself, paced around, and had chronic diarrhea. It took weeks to find food he would eat (Chows tend to be picky eaters, anyway) and every time we traveled from San Carlos to Tucson or Tucson to San Carlos, his stomach problems worsened. We figured that any change in setting must have made him think we were going to pass him off to someone else.

It took him more than four months to establish a bond of trust. Eventually, his stools returned to normal and when he wasn't playing, he acted like a "Chill Chow." He must have known then that he'd found his lifetime home. Trust is a two-way street. He used to try to bolt out the door when we first got him. He succeeded once and we had to tackle him on the sidewalk to stop him. Now, after nearly two years together, we know he won't run away. We even let him run loose on the beach occasionally when there aren't unfamiliar dogs or birds around.

Dozens of Mexican and American children have petted him on the head and a few people have asked to have photos taken with him. I always explain how to approach—he doesn't like fast movements or to be grabbed or touched by surprise on the butt or tail—and then the interactions usually go well. He has occasionally taken a dislike to a person or a dog for one reason or another, greeting them with a bark or a snarl instead of his normal Chief talk, which sounds a little like whining. But he's never bitten anyone and everyone who knows him thinks he's a wonderful dog.

Our neighbor, Kathryn, loves him so much, she requests time to visit him at the beach or even opportunities to walk him. And when he sees her outside, he whines and paces around, interpreting her every exit from her condo as a precursor to another Chief visit.

Whenever we get a "red" light when we go through customs in Nogales, Sonora after crossing the border, we have to pull off to the side and let the National Guard and customs agents examine what's in our vehicle. They always want to see Chief and pet him and largely forget about searching our car.

Chief has seen the dolphins up close a few times when I've paddled him around on the kayak. He turns to watch their dorsal fins rise above the surface and his ears perk up whenever he hears a loud, watery blowhole exhale. I wonder if the dolphins are happy for me, if they know that even though we lost one precious companion, a new one is bringing warmth and delight into our lives.

CHAPTER FORTY

Tucson, Arizona – February 2021

Days passed, with us still living mostly in isolation, splitting
our time between Tucson and San Carlos. Hikes offered
welcome respites from long days at home. We met Marion at
the Sabino Canyon parking lot one early afternoon with a plan
to hike to Seven Falls. I'd never done that hike before in the
many years I've been in the Tucson area.

After a major rain or after snowmelt, water rushes down
the valleys and even over parts of the main tram road. Deep
pools of water offer drinking spots for animals and oases for
overheated hikers. Due to recent snows, we expected to see
water in the canyons and pools.

Sabino Canyon is one of my favorite walking and hiking
places. Although this trail was new to me, I've walked on the
road and along other trails in the area hundreds of times. The
Santa Catalina Mountains, like many other mountains in the
Tucson area, including the Tortolita Mountains near our house,

are considered by geologists to be metamorphic core complexes or surface exposures of rocks from deep in the earth's crust.

The mountains and majestic cliffs of black-and-white-striped gneiss around us were created from the 1.4-billion-year-old Oracle Granite and the 50-million-year-old Wilderness Granite. Compressive forces raised these ancient rocks to the surface, enabling streams to carve out canyons and produce the amazing landscapes we enjoy today.

Many of the cliffs and hills around Sabino Canyon are forested with towering saguaro cactuses. The arms of the saguaros stretch up—sometimes 40 to 60 feet—into the sky, their ancient arms extending out and upward, except in rare instances when they grow into unusual shapes like a clutching hand or a curling spiral. Up close, holes in the trunks where cactus wrens nest are apparent. The birds know when it's safe to penetrate the columnar trunks—striped with rows of spikes—so they don't bleed the cactus to death.

Saguaro cacti are unique to the Sonoran Desert, which extends from southern Arizona into California and northern Sonora, México. Whenever we drive to San Carlos, we wind through hills and an amazing saguaro forest just outside of Magdalena, south of Nogales.

Enormous cardón cacti (Mexican giant cactus) replace the saguaros in the San Carlos area. Their arms sprout up from the ground instead of from a central trunk. I spotted another forest of saguaro cactus along 100—the route from Hermosillo to Kino Bay. There are forests of saguaros, forests of cardón cacti and then zones where the two types grow side-by-side. And I've seen a stray saguaro or two on the road to Miramar and along the Mex-15 bypass around Obregón.

Some 92,000 acres of saguaro forest are protected in the Saguaro National Park areas to the east and west of Tucson. Many saguaros are being relocated at record numbers from their rooting places as housing complexes replace acres and acres of natural desert. Knowing they get replanted is only a small consolation to me. Being transplanted into a block and cinder neighborhood must be a disappointment compared to the promise of growing old in the middle of a wild desert. And although it's illegal, some developers just knock them down.

Burgeoning temperatures in the Tucson and Phoenix metro areas, augmented by acres of pavement and new construction, create an unfavorable environment for the saguaro, inhibiting their ability to store water and photosynthesize.

A 2018 report by the National Park Service stated that climate change, invasive species, drought, and human activity are decreasing the population of new saguaro seedlings. Park Biologist Don Swann and co-author of the study spoke to an *AzCentral* reporter in June of 2020. He said that seedlings and juvenile cactus have been on the decline since the 1990s.

In the same article, Kevin Hultine, plant physiologist/ecophysiologist at the Desert Botanical Garden, reported that seedlings thrive better in their early decades when surrounded by mesquite, palo verde, and ironwood trees. These nurse trees provide shade and wind protection for nearby seedlings. When transplanted, they are more often surrounded by buffelgrass and other highly flammable invasive species, which put the saguaros at extreme risk of destruction by wildfire. Although volunteers cull these invasive grasses, the saguaros, like much of nature, remain at the mercy of human activity and climate change.

The hike to Seven Falls starts on paved road and becomes progressively more difficult. People wove around us and five minutes later, we passed other groups. I'd catch shreds of conversations until their voices faded into the wind. We started out in scorching heat until clouds rolled in, and the wind intensified.

We traversed narrow trails that followed or crossed streams of icy runoff. The water was clear as crystal and the sound of it pouring over rocks was soothing. I paused periodically to study our surroundings. I couldn't enjoy the view when walking without risking a fall.

We walked deeper and deeper into the valley until the metropolis of Tucson seemed to have disappeared. Suddenly, the trail angled upward and eventually, a V-shaped view of Tucson's buildings and roads appeared in the distance behind us. The trail hugged the side of a cliff and led us hundreds of feet above the stream valley.

Marion seemed in pleasant spirits, despite recent happenings. A hospital filled with COVID patients had left her stressed and burned out. Even though I avoided mentioning work, it seemed clear she was dealing with a lot. The good news was she'd gotten both of her COVID vaccines, and they were now available to most elderly Americans. Maybe soon, her job wouldn't be so difficult.

We turned a corner and there it was – an enormous multi-layered waterfall pouring over a precipice of 50-million-year-old granite to fill enormous pools of rock below. We were surrounded by rocks and cactus and tumbling water. Up high on the cliffs, there was little vegetation to obstruct our view.

We reached the pools at 3:30 PM. The icy wind barred me from plunging into the largest pool, but I shucked off my hiking boots and waded into the icy water wherever there was sand, avoiding the sheets of gneiss, which were slick with algae. My legs numbed within minutes. Two-inch-long fish swam around me. The cold water heightened my senses, made me feel incredibly alive. I had recently started taking cold water swims, showers, and ice baths, after reading Wim Hof's book on the benefits of exposing yourself to cold water. Instead of dreading these cold dips, I now craved them.

I watched people hike up toward the top of the falls and disappear. There are other pools up there, Chris said. We didn't want to finish our hike after dark, so reluctantly we began our return trip. Lost in thoughts, I flashed back to the two times I had hiked the Inca Trail — first in 1996 with a group of friends — and a second time in 2006 with Chris and a group of other tourists. Those hikes had been so exhilarating.

The chill in the air on our Seven Falls hike reminded me so much of those walks through the Andes. I felt the same thrill of vitality, the same brush of cold on my cheeks while my body warmed me like a furnace with every step. I felt grateful to be out in the wild natural world hiking with two people I loved dearly.

At the end of our hike, we enjoyed a chilly outdoor picnic at a table near the parking lot. Chris and I had bought salads, cheeses, and goodies from Trader Joe's and several La Croix to drink.

While we savored a meal, Marion mentioned that she wanted to take a trip to Colombia. Maybe we could go together, she suggested. We'd both heard it had become safer for tourists in recent years. It had blossomed as the latest wonderland for outdoor adventurers on a budget.

That day of hiking felt like an exotic adventure after too many days confined to the house. And talking about travel made me imagine an almost-normal life. Chris and I might be eligible to get our vaccines in a month or two. Then maybe we'd be able to choose a destination and fly there like we once had. It was fun to dream.

But until then, we had parks in Tucson and our beautiful beach in San Carlos where we could connect to nature and experience the serenity that only the outdoors can bring.

CHAPTER FORTY-ONE

San Carlos, México - May 7, 2021

Chris and I had both gotten our two vaccines. Life wasn't exactly normal, but we could socialize with our family and friends now in relative calm. Our condo complex in México had survived the tumult. I'd been worried when the complex was largely deserted, that it would be vandalized or robbed. Weeks before the pandemic started, we'd hired a new general manager since our former one had left after giving his two-week's notice.

None of the board members had seen the pandemic coming when we were faced with needing to hire a new manager and fast. I was a member of the HOA Oversight Committee at the time. We discussed spending a big chunk of change hiring a recruiter. But I kept wondering…If the last recruiter brought us José, why should we hire him again?

I prayed to know that there was a right person to fill this position who would bless our community and find the leadership opportunity at Bahía Delfín to be a blessing. I believe

God listens to honest prayers. And he often answers them, as he did in this instance.

We decided to publish the job locally. Two candidates applied. The first man we interviewed—who arrived a few minutes late—had a powerful, athletic frame and an irritating ego. He had worked with a seafood company for many years. He knew how to manage people, he said. Managing a small place like Bahía Delfín would be easy after managing the team of people he'd overseen before, he boasted. At the end of the interview, he concluded by saying "You need me." Like a hole in the head, I thought.

The next candidate, Roberto, shook our hands and greeted us with kind words and a smile that seemed genuine and from the heart—not just forced muscles stretching skin. A former water company executive, he asked many thoughtful questions about the needs of our community.

Our board unanimously agreed to hire him. A year later, he has time and time again showed himself to be downright heroic.

Stay at home orders for Sonora were issued just days after he was hired and only a skeleton staff was permitted on the property. Roberto had to get special permission from the local authorities to have two guards at night to keep the property safer.

Early on, he identified serious problems. The most significant one involved our water treatment plant. Water to the condos was being directed by only one pump—instead of the normal four—and that pump did not meet the proper specifications. Roberto had to order four new pumps, which took several weeks to arrive.

Nothing happens fast in México, especially during a pandemic. In the meantime, we had regular water outages. Roberto often had to call in workers in the middle of the night.

People were upset. But what choice was there? He did the best he could. And in the end, he solved the problem.

After restrictions loosened, workers were allowed to return, beaches opened, and owners ventured back down. Initially, the "essential travel" restrictions applied to travel in both directions. But soon the Mexican government allowed everyone in because businesses were crippled by diminished tourism. Canadian condo owners still couldn't come down because of U.S. border restrictions.

The Bahía Delfín workers seemed happier and more productive than they had been under José's oversight. One day when sitting under my beach tent, I heard Roberto talking to Gabriel and Lupita and another housekeeper. They were all talking and laughing together in an easy, comfortable manner.

Roberto is a hard worker and he's kind and friendly to everyone. I think of him as our Bahía Delfín angel. God's gift to all of us. I believe all of us can be Divine gifts to others if we allow ourselves to be. We can bring blessings to our family, our friends, people who work with or for us, and even people we see at the grocery store. And we can do our part for the natural world as well. The animals we share this planet with also need us to be mindful and considerate of them.

CHAPTER FORTY-TWO

Hermosillo, México – May 18, 2021

Chris and I had finally obtained our Mexican driver's licenses. Soon after, we bought a car in Hermosillo, giving us the freedom to drive outside the free zones (between Nogales and Guaymas and in Baja California), the only areas where permanent residents are allowed to drive American cars.

We paid for the Mazda CX-5 with a credit card since wire transfers from the U.S. were problematic. The small SUV has served us well—delivering comfort, reliability, and good gas mileage. In addition to making many trips back to Tucson, we've driven our CX-5 to Alamos, Rosarito, Kino Bay, Los Mochis, and Mazatlán. And Chief seems quite content to ride along, sprawled out and relaxed on the cushy leather back seat.

I enjoyed our trip to Rosarito, in northern Baja, the most. We drove there last summer after a week in Solana Beach with my stepson and stepdaughter and her family. It was barely an hour's drive south of San Diego—suddenly we were across the border and the glamour of southern California with its mansions and beautiful greenery faded away and the untidy structures of Tijuana and barren brown ground appeared.

Traveling to México after being in the U.S. for a while is often jarring, as is making the transition south to north. The too-fast-paced-life and the lack of connection between people throws me off balance whenever I visit the U.S. The potholes, street vendors, and window washers that rush up to your car in towns, and the trash and discarded piles of construction waste alarm me whenever I return to México.

We'd rented an Airbnb house right on the water. The landmark we were instructed to look for near the turn off into the neighborhood in El Morro was the Christ of the Sacred Heart—a 75-foot-tall statue of Jesus on top of a barren hilltop. Staying outside of Rosarito turned out to be a blessing. Traffic in town came to a complete standstill the weekend we were there, and I spotted mostly California license plates. Everyone seemed to be flooding south of the border to visit family.

We drove under a white cement arch and entered a code to gain entrance to the area. A gravel road led toward the coast and a neighborhood of a dozen or so houses. The homes differed vastly—there were modern, white, blocky structures beside quaint brick, stone, and wooden buildings. Wooden gates and large trees blocked our view of the homes near our rental.

We pulled up in front of a little country house—wooden and painted in cheerful colors. The owner, Laurie, was waiting for us and showed us around before leaving to visit family in Southern California. Since she lived in the home when not renting it, it had everything we needed.

The house was perched high above the Pacific Ocean on rocky cliffs. The view was tremendous—from the brick and stone patio, we saw the vast ocean, some rocky islands, and long stretches of coastline north and south of us. At high tide, the waves pounded at the cliffs, rattling the sliding doors and windows, awakening us during the night. Laurie suggested we slip coasters into the gaps in the windows to minimize the vibration. We also had to be careful with Chief out on the patio because it ended abruptly with a dangerous precipice—no fence. But everything else about staying in the house was perfect.

Laurie had collected fresh eggs from her local coop and put them in the refrigerator for us. Never has an omelet or scrambled eggs tasted so good. The whole house was decorated like a little country cottage, with walls and window shutters painted in bright colors and frilly curtains trimming windows. The furniture was well-worn but cozy and comfortable.

Every morning, we drove about 15 minutes south on the winding Pacific Highway to La Misión beach to walk Chief. Heavy fog hung over the beach. The air was chilly and humid. There were houses nested in the hills on the other side of the freeway, above a large estuary. Vendors sold food and produce from a row of thatched roof shacks. Most of the businesses remained shuttered in the early morning hours.

There was a forlornness about the place that is hard to describe. Maybe it was the fog, the almost black color of the sand riddled with trash or the muddiness of the water.

La Misión beach contrasted starkly with the Del Mar dog beach where we'd taken Chief every morning. He'd run free, chasing other dogs, sometimes collapsing into the sand, exhausted, to watch other dogs retrieve balls thrown by owners into the water. An orderly arrangement of homes decorated the nearby hills. Volleyball nets sat in tidy rows in the sand, waiting for the parties who had reserved them to arrive. A tall lifeguard chair—vacant in the early morning hours—offered a view of the estuary and a stretch of the Pacific beyond it. No debris soiled the pale sand.

The Del Mar residents projected a relaxed and privileged air. Most were so wealthy, they'd probably never worried about money or where their next meal would come from like far too many people south of the border. One woman told me her dog was from México and when I asked if she lived there, her eyes widened with alarm. "Oh, no. Someone brings them up from there." She said the word "there" as if her dog had been transported from a prison, not a country less than an hour south of whatever mansion she lived in where millions of Americans had comfortably retired.

I enjoy visiting southern California but would never want to live there. I don't like the traffic, the arrogance, the prices. And the state has too many rules. Everywhere, signs are posted. And whenever we trade our RCI points for the Sand Pebbles Resort in Solana Beach, we are required to sign a nearly 20-page document before checking in. We can't be trusted to act appropriately on our own. That's one of the blessings of México. There aren't too many rules. You are treated like an adult instead of a five-year-old.

During the four days we spent in Rosarito, I vacillated between enjoying every new experience, such as taking an hour-long swim at a pool at a zip line park surrounded by a jungle of trees and flowering bushes, and longing to be somewhere familiar.

Vacations are lovely. Being home in San Carlos is even better. There's comfort in sleeping on my own pillow, cooking in our kitchen, being surrounded by familiar artwork and décor, comfort in the routine of daily affairs, comfort in knowing the sea is there for me to swim in every morning after I awaken.

CHAPTER FORTY-THREE

San Carlos, México –February 4, 2022

The previous winter, I attempted cold-water swims without a wetsuit after reading Wim Hof's book, *The Wim Hof Method*. I was attracted by the health benefits and the possibility that I could overcome my cold water intolerance and maybe one day tackle one or more of the seven marathon open water swims known as the Oceans Seven—such as the English Channel or the Catalina Channel.

So far this year, I've swum up to 28 minutes without a wetsuit in water ranging from 58 to 62 degrees Fahrenheit. Sometimes when I'm in Tucson, I take ice baths or cold showers. But there's nothing like a winter sea swim.

That day, the sea felt colder than ever during my morning swim. So cold, that my feet burned painfully afterward under hot water in the shower. It reminded me how I felt after skiing many years ago in Ohio, Michigan, Canada, and Colorado—

when my feet were on the cusp of frostbite and then began to thaw indoors.

Entering cold water makes my muscles seize up in shock. I cry out when my body first hits the water. I have to remind myself to breathe. After several strokes, my skin and muscles numb and tingly warmth envelopes my body. My face still feels icy cold. Soon, I experience the normal elation of moving through water. When I begin to feel slightly confused or lightheaded, that's my signal to end the swim.

Even though I'm always freezing after a non-wetsuit swim, I feel incredibly alive and joyous. All my senses are heightened—my mind feels clear and crisp as does my view of the sea and volcanic mountains all around. More than once, I've shouted with glee while sprinting from the water up the beach. Most of the time, this happy high lasts for hours. I wish everyone could experience it at least once.

Last week, two male dolphins wove back and forth in front of me when I swam. They were so close I had to slow to a breaststroke not to touch them.

On this morning, I didn't see them until they were right under me since an algal bloom had dropped the water visibility down to almost nothing. It made me nervous, not knowing where they were.

I saw turbulent water all around me, as if they were moving fast within inches of my face. The third day they did this, I said out loud underwater that they were scaring me. And I wondered...Were they annoyed with me?

Did they know everyone in the complex seemed to be getting COVID? Did they blame me for the murky water? These winter algal blooms are likely connected to the sewage flowing into the sea from a few places in San Carlos and everywhere in Guaymas. Maybe they wonder why we're so careless, why humans leave a damaging imprint everyplace they go.

For more than a week afterward, I didn't encounter the dolphins up close. Maybe they wanted to avoid me. Or maybe they sensed the tremor in my trust.

CHAPTER FORTY-FOUR

San Carlos, México – August 2017-April 2022

Moving to México, I faced the normal chaos of relocation, along with the challenge of a new language, and a major cultural shift. I found some of these experiences exciting. Others felt like they crashed down on me like a rogue wave. I do have one advantage, though. When I moved to Peru in the 1990s, I had no home in the States to run back to. Since we still own a small house in Arizona, I can head north if I need a break. And I often do during times I prefer to avoid crowds—like *Semana Santa*. But not every expatriate has this option.

Sitting under my beach tent reading, I often glance up to watch families gathering at the beach. I've watched children play tag, throw seaweed and sand at each other, build sandcastles, play soccer, and splash around with big floaty toys. Family members helped unsteady elderly parents walk across the sand. I've seen four generations sitting together, eating pizzas and meals brought in Styrofoam containers (and I've always wished that Styrofoam could be banned). I've watched teenage boys and girls take selfies and group photos and drink more beers than I could ever imagine drinking. Before leaving, they pick up every scrap of trash. And I've felt very happy and content watching them.

There had been other weekends at the beach where I heard the roar of Jet Skis just offshore and smelled gasoline fumes mixed with nearby cigarette smoke and toxic perfume. People all around me played blaring, staticky music from cars or tall speakers until I felt an anxious fight-or-flight impulse to run away from all the noise and chaos.

I have walked down to my tent to find dozens of people camped out. Sometimes, I just turn and walk away. On other occasions, I explain that these are my belongings and ask them to vacate. When people set up right beside me and blare their music as if I weren't even there and I see the beach becoming littered with trash, I feel lonely and disillusioned. Why do they have to be so noisy? Why can't they care about nature? Or a fellow human being?

My yoga teacher training leader, Lucas, despite his faults, shared words of wisdom I'll never forget. He said with practice, we could be content in any place, under any circumstances. We could learn to block out noise and discord and find harmony inside ourselves. In the U.S., my neighbor's home-based construction company work drove me insane. Now in México, loud music, car alarms, and roaring engines sometimes steal my sense of peace.

We live on the west side of the complex beside the public beach. On weekends and holidays, blaring music often makes our floors vibrate and sends me rushing to grab my noise-cancelling headphones.

There have been days my heart rate skyrocketed the instant I heard some disturbing noise. I've always experienced very intense sensitivity to loud noises. They tend to induce panic and anger. When it happens, I have to pause, take several slow, deep breaths, and tell myself I don't have to react. I would pray for peace of mind or go deep into a meditation and eventually find that the music or voices will fade into the background and not bother me as much anymore. In my consciousness, I make the choice whether to remain in harmony or descend into misery.

There have been days when I feel overwhelmed and have to wear noise-cancelling headphones and run our HVAC system fan all day to block all the chaos out until I can bring myself back to a calm state. I've even escaped to another location on occasions where the trauma from noise became too overwhelming.

Noisy, inconsiderate people can be found in every country and on every continent. And in every country, you can also encounter people who are mindful of their neighbors as well as the natural world, who don't treat animals and the land and sea they live in as things to be conquered or exploited.

I had a long talk with a good Mexican friend, Verónica, recently outside on her balcony. She says Mexicans are much more easy-going than Americans. Mexicans—herself included—find many Americans to be inflexible and uptight. I agreed with what she said.

If Verónica goes to meet a friend at a restaurant and that friend shows up 30 minutes late, oh, well. If she goes to a friend's house for dinner and they end up serving dinner at eight instead of six thirty, she doesn't like it if it's a work night because she's an early morning exerciser like me, but she doesn't let it throw her off kilter.

Most people in México prefer to stay up late and sleep in. Meanwhile, I go to bed before nine and awaken every morning by five. I eat and exercise and sleep on a schedule as recommended by health coach, Debbie Waidl. Her recommendations, combined with my faith and daily prayers, have enabled me to experience wellness again. This is a small gift I offer myself. And I feel I'm worthy of it. For now, I dine with friends who eat at similar times and turn down invitations that are likely to throw me out of balance.

There's so much I admire about the Mexican culture. For instance, Mexicans see amazing beauty in a pregnant woman's body. Pregnant women often come to the beach in glamorous dresses, bellies exposed, and accompanied by photographers. The other night my husband and I watched a woman decked out in a dress made entirely of neon pink feathers. I could never imagine wearing anything like that outfit. But I was fascinated and wondered how my own pregnancy experiences would have differed if people in my culture valued the pregnant body more.

I worked as a fitness coordinator for a gym while pregnant with my daughter. I taught water exercise until my due date. As my belly expanded, I started wearing a swimsuit with an exercise bra under it. A bit of my whale white belly peeked out below the bra top and above the very overstretched neckline of the suit.

Every morning in the locker room, one dear friend, Marylou, regaled me with stories about her first pregnancy and how her belly had become a convenient "table." Two other co-workers became pregnant at the same time, and we joked about the gym water fountain inducing pregnancy.

Not all my pregnancy experiences were positive. Students eyeing my bump asked me how much longer I would teach. And I felt — quite frankly — dreadful. I didn't feel strong, firm, and athletic. I felt clunky and awkward. I experienced rollercoaster moods and waves of nausea. I had stopped teaching land classes and now taught only water exercise. After teaching a class, I wanted to lie down and go to sleep.

Late in my pregnancy, I went to retrieve the time sheets for payroll. Someone had written "Too fat to teach" on mine. These words landed like a punch. I felt awkward moving about in my pregnant body. But now I felt ugly, too.

My self-image then was fragile, like the sand dollars I sometimes find on the beach. I hadn't yet recovered from my years living with my parents where my father criticized my eating habits and weight.

I've moved past caring what people do or don't like about my body, my lifestyle, or anything else. It's essential to establish your own values and choices—independent of others' expectations. Otherwise, it's impossible to find contentment or to live your best life—whatever that means for you.

I now think the pregnancy bias I suffered is abominable. A new life was forming in that 'fat' belly. And she is precious, not repulsive.

Mexicans live a celebratory life. Days off work happen on about ten national holidays. Dozens of other small holidays are celebrated. In addition to the special photos taken for pregnancy, I've witnessed countless other special events at the beach. Gender reveals, when the crowd of friends learns whether an impending baby will be a boy or a girl, are rife with cookouts, photo sessions, and the launching of fireworks that spew out blue or pink smoke. *Quinceañeras* are birthday celebrations for 15-year-old girls. I often see them in frilly red dresses that look like ball gowns. The girls pose in front of the camera, bouquets of red roses in their hands. I find rose petals strewn across the sand the mornings after when we walk Chief.

One day a young Mexican man with a large family group asked if he could pet Chief. I soon learned his family had come to San Carlos from different cities all over México. They were celebrating his sister's birthday. But sadly, without her still here on earth. She had died of COVID the previous year, he said. My eyes filled with tears when he told me how they would spend the weekend sharing fond memories of his sister instead.

Often in the U.S., people urge their friends and family to move on after someone dies. A writer friend once told me that her family members chided her whenever she mentioned her dead spouse. The poor man had committed suicide. My friend died suddenly last year. I don't know the details, but I often wonder if she missed him too much and couldn't cope with the subsequent isolation and disconnection that resulted from people's judgment and lack of compassion. Every person needs to be understood, cared for, and, yes, touched. I think most Mexicans feel loved and cherished, surrounded as they are by large, loving families.

I'm not a fan of the Mexican penchant for noise. Mexican beaches in general are party places. Music from tower-style speakers blares in the afternoons and into the wee hours on weekends and holidays. Revelers have no interest in savoring the sounds of the birds or the waves. They converse as they float in the sea—beer in hand—but most of those cans and bottles never make it out of the water and into garbage cans.

Big Band music from a Guadalupe Festival during a December visit to Mazatlán made our ears ring, even after retreating to our hotel room. Chris has adapted to México over the course of the past year or so. He practices Spanish daily, joined a beach volleyball group, found a running buddy, and is serving on the Bahía Delfín HOA board.

Chris asked me, annoyed, but still maintaining his sense of humor, "What is it you like about México? It's hot, noisy, there are strong smells, and everything is total chaos."

I laughed and shook my head. I told him that México brought back memories of my time in Peru. But even there I hadn't much liked the fireworks in the middle of the night, the vendors that shouted, "*papas, zanahorias, cebollas*" at the crack of dawn when I was still asleep. There were days in Peru when I wished I were somewhere else and there are days when I'm in México — such as that hot, noisy day in Mazatlán — where I wanted nothing more than to be instantly transported to our Arizona house, Harry Potter style with a portkey.

But in some ways, we are isolated from real México in this condo complex, especially during the week when the public beach isn't crowded. Because of our lifestyle, we prefer to live where there are quiet hours and other American-like norms are practiced. And it's a haven to recover from culture shock until I'm ready to venture back out to experience more of México and its people. I still have much to learn and understand.

CHAPTER FORTY-FIVE

San Carlos, México – March 10, 2022

"Can we now allow ourselves to entertain the possibility that
the supernatural, the divine, and the magical may all underlie
our physical world?"
Neurosurgeon Allan J. Hamilton

Church isn't where I find God. I draw close to my
Father/Mother walking the Inca Trail, gazing up at a sea of
stars in a dune field in the Atacama Desert, hiking in the Santa
Catalina Mountains, meditating in a New Mexico pine forest,
biking through the Swiss Alps with snow-capped mountains all
around me, and swimming with the dolphins in the Sea of
Cortez. Every experience reminds me of the beauty of this earth
that God created. I feel a connection to God — and compelled to
love and take care of all that our dear Lord has created.

It's my daughter, Marion's birthday today. I prayed for her
and other family members during my sea swim. I pray for

people every morning while I propel myself through the water. The dolphins swam around me the whole time. It wasn't just one or two of them today. The whole pod accompanied me. First, the guy with the line of curved scratches on his back between his dorsal fin and flukes. He's been swimming with me almost every day lately. Yesterday, he seemed upset when I returned to shore. He swam almost to the beach after I exited. I don't know how to say in dolphin speak, "It was fun swimming with you, but I've got to get out because I'm on the verge of hypothermia."

He circled around me, cut in front of me, so close, his tail and sometimes his dorsal fin was just inches from my face and hands. He rolled over on his back and glided around and under me showing me his white belly. Once, when he returned, a huge garland of seaweed was draped around one of his pectoral fins. Did he pick it up intentionally? Was this part of the game? He even opened his mouth wide and showed me the long line of blunt white teeth. And then three others appeared. They were all around me. I saw fins everywhere. And then they kept swimming underneath me, their bodies close enough to touch. I could see every white scratch on each of their gray bodies.

What inspires a dolphin that can easily swim 25 mph to drift along with me at my slow pace. Curiosity? The desire to connect with another species of living being? Whenever they glide beneath me, a small flick of the fluke propels them beyond my swimming speed. They're so strong and powerful, so precise and coordinated.

I didn't notice the owner of RADA SC video recording my swim. But he later posted a video on Facebook of the one dolphin gliding alongside me. He referred to me as a *muchacho* — a young man. Soon some friends identified me, the "young man" who was actually a 59-year-old woman. Their tags brought the video to my attention.

Two weeks later this video post had attracted 144,000 likes, 9,600 shares, 1,700 comments, and 6 million views. If only the viewers could see what I saw—all these dolphins from inches away. The thousands of comments from people in both English and Spanish show how fascinated people are by nature and the possibility of connecting to a living being of a different species. The Spanish comments mentioned have been translated.

Victoria had heard people rave about the beauty of San Carlos and expressed her gratitude for the sharing of the video. "God bless you a lot," she said.

Cecy wrote, "Beautiful creatures that our Father Mother made."

Carmen said, "How lucky and how beautiful to be escorted by a wonderful dolphin."

Milita said, "This beautiful dolphin is taking care of him."

Verónica said, "What a great joy to swim in the company of such a grand and noble creature."

Eva said, "Thanks for sharing…God bless you."

Another poster described the dolphins as protective angels.

Many people wanted to know where San Carlos was so they could meet these dolphins. Incredible, marvelous, and beautiful were common adjectives used in posts. Concerns for the environment were expressed. Some shared their own experiences with the dolphins during visits to San Carlos.

Joze said, "I hope people realize it is not a pool," and then went on to mention all the dangerous creatures that lurk in the sea.

He wasn't alone. Many other posters expressed their fear of sharks and the dangers of swimming in open water. To me, this spoke to our innate fear of what we don't understand. I'm not afraid of the sea anymore because I immerse myself in it every day. I feel a sense of harmony with the natural world because I spend so much time outside. I wouldn't engage in unwise swimming adventures like island-to-island swims without kayak support, but I often swim parallel to the coast alone.

Many people spend their days confined inside the walls of their homes and offices. A large body of water or a dense forest to some are places to be feared and avoided, rather than sanctuaries or places of renewal. And others who visit beautiful places drown out the life-renewing nature sounds with deafening music. They get freaked out by silence, I suppose because they are so unused to it. I wish everyone could know the peace and harmony I experience when I'm in a quiet space connecting with nature—whether it's a sea, forest, or the mountains.

Eduardo wrote in Spanish, "That swimmer must have some spiritual peace or tranquility for that beautiful creature to accompany him swimming ... Incredible and it must be emphasized that this dolphin is not domesticated, what a beautiful case."

I can only hope the dolphins choose to swim with me because it uplifts them as much as it does me.

EPILOGUE

March-April, 2022 – San Carlos, México

"Through the eyes of animals, we see ourselves correctly."
People of the Sea - W. Michael Gear and Kathleen O'Neal Gear.

I waded into the water before 7 AM. Seeing movement in the shallows, I paused my shuffling to wait for the sting ray to glide by. The water is slowly warming. I can swim for more than 40 minutes without a wetsuit now. Some days in the spring and the fall, when there's a large temperature difference between the air and the water, fog rolls in. It often happens suddenly — I'll see a layer on the horizon and minutes later it advances. When it engulfs me during a swim, the mountains disappear, and I see only gray water and a whirl of white and feel that I've been transported to a fantasy world.

Yesterday, howling wind whipped around our building. Today, the wind had diminished, but the swells were huge.

All through the swim, I felt my body rise and fall over the waves. Wind rippled the waves and the water looked midnight blue, as it often does in the early morning. I took a breath every three strokes while I swam freestyle. Whenever I turned my head to breathe on the seaward side, I saw big swells rolling my way.

Toward the end of my swim, I looked toward shore and saw a woman pointing. I turned to see two dark fins glinting under the sunlight. Their dorsal fins look black in the sunlight and gray underwater. I swam toward them and saw turbulent water all around me. Then two gray bodies glided fast underneath me. I alternated between breaststroke and freestyle. I spoke to them, wishing the dolphins good morning and asking how they were. I saw fins on all sides of me, bodies cruising underneath me, more turbulence.

I have been swimming with these dolphins for five years now. They've observed me as much as I've observed them. I wonder if one of them wrote a book, what they would say about me. What they would say about Danielle. What they would say about the dozens of kayakers that interact with them on a regular basis.

Animals are drawn to kind people. Dogs walk over to them, cats sleep in their laps, birds don't fly away when they walk by. My son is an animal whisperer. He needs little explanation on Chief's care when we go on vacation, because he seems to sense what to do with him. I never have any concerns that Chief will be unhappy in my son's care because he trots to the door with delight, tail curled up high in the air every time Keith comes for dinner or a visit.

"Through the eyes of animals, we see ourselves correctly," reads a line in the novel about North American Paleoindians, *People of the Sea*, by W. Michael Gear and Kathleen O'Neal Gear. They also say that people see our bodies while animals see through to our souls. And it's true. Your dog doesn't care whether you're wearing makeup or stylish clothes or if you're popular. He cares about your heart. Our dog seems to like me more on some days than others. I'm starting to use that much more as a barometer for self-improvement than trying to fit in with humans.

When our dog nods his head as if agreeing with something I said or the dolphins choose to swim near me, I know I must be sending good energy out to the world.

I rushed up the beach to grab my towel, glancing wide-eyed at the dramatic landscape all around me and thinking that San Carlos is one of the most beautiful places in the world. Even *National Geographic* agrees with me. The magazine cited the town's El Mirador as one of the top 10 ocean views in the world.

Unfortunately, San Carlos is increasingly becoming the beach place in Sonora to party, with more emphasis on drunkenness and hedonism than preserving the beauty of the natural environment. Another *Semana Santa*, bringing tens of thousands of visitors, has come and gone. Weeks later, mountains of trash and human waste left behind after the celebration were still being removed. The damage to the environment is hard to quantify.

Every Monday morning, following the weekend's festivities, we walk Chief and pick up discarded cans, bottles, cups, Styrofoam food containers, and so much other junk. The five minutes it would take to bag up this garbage and put it in its proper place is apparently too great of a kindness to extend to the dolphins, fish, birds, and other creatures that live in this space. Ingesting plastic results in the death of numerous marine creatures and countless others end up entangled in ropes, plastic beer can rings, and fishing line. CRRIFS receives reports weekly about entangled turtles and sea lions.

Trucks and ATVs race up and down the beaches. They spin their tires when they get stuck and often terrorize people walking the beach. They flatten birds and compact the sand above sea turtle nests, giving the hatchlings little chance to emerge from the nest. If they do get out, they often die on their trek to the sea, tumbling down and getting stuck in the deep grooves of tire tracks, unable to escape.

For this reason, the CRRIFS turtle team members received authorization from the Mexican government to remove threatened nests from the beach, preserving the eggs until the hatching date in an incubation facility.

Fisherman poach sea turtle eggs from the beach and capture and kill Olive Ridleys and other species of sea turtles, despite their protected statuses. Shrimp boats drag the ocean bottom, destroying reefs. Many turtles, dolphins, porpoises, and sea lions get entangled in nets or fishing line. Humans continue to pose the biggest threat to most marine species.

Developers are constructing high-rise hotels and homes in places that were once animal habitats, rife with desert plants and dunes. Rumors are circulating that structures may even be built within the boundaries of the El Soldado Estuary, which is a nursery for thousands of marine species, supposedly under environmental protection by the Mexican government.

Many articles have been published illuminating widespread sewage leaks in San Carlos and Guaymas and how for the burgeoning population, a full-scale sewage treatment plant is necessary for both towns rather than the settling lagoons relied on now. Local developers and public officials don't seem to grasp the concept — or choose to ignore the idea — of sustainable development.

More and more boat owners chase the dolphin pods. They play loud music and shout at them. The boat captains don't know how to safely interact and sometimes the dolphins are sliced by their propeller blades—I've seen evidence of these injuries firsthand. People race Jet Skis across the water on weekends, terrifying swimmers, annoying people on the beach with the noise and the gas fumes, and striking unwary sea turtles.

In ten years, perhaps many of the people who moved to San Carlos to enjoy the incredible beauty of the area will have packed up for another, more peaceful place. My husband and I may be among them.

And someday *that* sanctuary may be ruined by careless visitors and developers. It's sad to consider. Especially, since our dolphin friends don't have that luxury. This is the sea where they live and if it's destroyed, they will perish. We humans go about our business, so many of us in denial that we will eventually face our own day of reckoning.

Today, San Carlos is my home, my husband's home, Chief's home. And this moment is the only time on Earth that's guaranteed. I will listen to what God wants me to do with each precious moment. For now, I teach yoga, volunteer with a team to help the sea turtles, write, savor friendships, and pick up trash. And I live by the sea.

As I look out at the wide expanse of blue-green water, I'm already imagining my next swim. Maybe if conditions are right, I'll see the dark flash of a dorsal fin under the rising sun. I can't wait for my next precious encounter with my bottlenose dolphin friends.

ACKNOWLEDGEMENTS

Writing *Swimming with Dolphins* was no small project! Without support, publishing this book wouldn't have been possible.

I wish to thank Jennifer J. Stewart for the many hours she dedicated to editing *Swimming with Dolphins*. Her corrections and recommendations really helped bring this book to life and for that, I am eternally grateful.

I also wish to thank my dear husband, Chris Ferko, for the many hours he spent reading chapters and making suggestions on how to improve them. In some cases, he even remembered an event with greater clarity than I, which helped me write it better the second time around. Thanks, Chris, for always being there for me.

REFERENCES/RECOMMENDED READING

Bregel, Emily. "Sewage crisis continues in popular Sonoran beach town." *The Arizona Daily Star* and *Tucson.com*. last updated June 20, 2022.
https://tucson.com/news/local/sewage-crisis-continues-in-popular-sonoran-beach-town/article_d608911c-ed01-11ec-b915-cba38457dbcc.html

Caché von Fettweis, Yvonne and Robert Townsend Warneck (1998). *Mary Baker Eddy: Christian Healer*. Amplified Edition. The Christian Science Publishing Society.

Casey, Susan (2015). *Voices in the Ocean: A Journey into the Wild and Haunting World of Dolphins*. Anchor Books.

Charles, Krista. "Whales and dolphins can resist cancer and their DNA reveals why." *New Scientist*. February 24, 2021.

https://www.newscientist.com/article/2268865-whales-and-dolphins-can-resist-cancer-and-their-dna-reveals-why/

Cruz, Chris. "Filipino diver thinks dolphins saved him from the 2004 tsunami." Discovery TV Network on Facebook [Video]. March 26, 2018. https://www.facebook.com/watch/?v=2148668771817619

Dawson Cook, Susan. "Back Injury Quickly Healed." *Christian Science Sentinel*. vol 123, no. 2, January 11, 2021.

Dawson Cook, Susan. "The Right Employee Found." *The Christian Science Journal*. vol. 140, no. 8, August 1, 2022.

Eddy, Mary Baker. (1994). *Science and Health with Key to the Scriptures*. Christian Science Board of Directors, Boston, Massachusetts.

Ehlrich, Pippa, and James Reed, directors (2020). *My Octopus Teacher*. Netflix Original Documentary film.

Gear, W. Michael and Kathleen O'Neal Gear (1993). *People of the Sea*. McMillan, Forge Books.

Herman, L. M., Richards, D. G. and Wolz, J. P. (1984). "Comprehension of sentences by bottlenosed dolphins." *Cognition*. vol. 16, pp. 129-219.

Hof, Wim. (2020). *The Wim Hof Method: Activate Your Full Human Potential*. Sounds True Publishing, Louisville, CO.

Iyengar, B.K.S. (2002). *Light on the Yoga Sutras of Patanjali.* Thorsons new edition.

King James Version Bible (1817). 1 John 4:6-8.

Kirkwood, Brandon. April 14, 2020. "Study: 90 percent of dolphins killed by fishing." *Vegan News* https://vegannews.press/2020/04/14/dophin-bycatch-study/

Krol, Debra Utacia. "With the saguaro cactus start to disappear from parts of the Southwest?" *AzCentral.* June 18, 2010. https://www.azcentral.com/story/news/local/arizona-environment/2020/06/18/saguaro-cactus-imperiled-climate-change-and-humans/3000183001/

Montgomery, Sy (2016). *The Soul of the Octopus.* Atria Books. New York, New York.

O'Barry, Ric. (2022). "End the Senseless Slaughter in Taiji." Accessed April 2, 2022. https://www.dolphinproject.com/take-action/save-japan-dolphins/

Reiss, Diana (2011). *The Dolphin in the Mirror: Exploring Dolphin Minds and Saving Dolphin Lives.* Mariner Books.

Satchidananda, Sri Swami. (2012). *The Yoga Sutras of Patanjali.* Integral Yoga Publications, Buckingham, Virginia.

Witherington, Blair and Dawn Witherington. *Our Sea Turtles: A Practical Guide for the Atlantic and Gulf, from Canada to México.* Pineapple Press, Inc. Sarasota, Florida. 2015.

Made in the USA
Las Vegas, NV
07 October 2023

78737729R00164